american
TELEVISION
genres

american TELEVISION genres

Stuart M. Kaminsky
with Jeffrey H. Mahan

Nelson-Hall nh Chicago

Library of Congress Cataloging in Publication Data

Kaminsky, Stuart M.
American television genres.

Bibliography: p.
Includes index.
1. Television programs–United States–History and criticism. I. Mahan, Jeffrey H. II. Title.
PN1992.3.U5K26 1984 791.45'75'0973 84-1022
ISBN 0-8304-1084-8 (cloth)
ISBN 0-88229-828-3 (paper)

Reprinted 1986, 1988

Manufactured in the United States of America

10 9 8 7 6 5 4 3

TM The paper used in this book meets the minimum requirements of American National Standard for Information Sciences—Permanence of Paper for Printed Library Materials, ANSI Z39.48-1984.

CONTENTS

PREFACE

American Television Genres attempts to explore some of the ways of studying our most popular form of entertainment and information. Even a cursory glance at the table of contents of this book will show that we have neither planned nor delivered a comprehensive catalog of television genres and ways of dealing with them. To do so would require a massive encyclopedia that would quickly be outdated as the genres change. What we have undertaken instead is to indicate a number of problems in dealing with popular television and specific means of examining the issue of genre, using a limited number of examples. It is our hope that the approaches dealt with will provide the reader with the means to move on to other examples, other genres, other concerns.

The reader should not think that in each chapter we are prescribing the *definitive* way of looking at a particular issue or genre. Rather, we have proposed *one* way of doing so which allows us to raise particular questions about the television show being considered. Someone else might choose to apply a different methodology to the specific genre being considered and hence would be led to pursue different questions. Or one might apply a methodology proposed here with one genre to a different genre. Either of these would be a potentially profitable approach to the study of television.

This leads to the second essential point about this book. We have not attempted to set up either a hierarchy of genres or of shows within a genre. We do not claim that science-fiction tales are "better than" soap opera or that "The Rockford Files" is the quintessential detective show. Such decisions are matters of individual taste, and we are not interested in imposing our personal preferences simply because we have the forum of the printed page. The reader is fully capable of deciding what genres and examples he or she likes. What we are interested in is presenting some means of exploring television genres that, we hope, will help the reader to think critically about the medium. Thus, this presentation should be of equal interest to the reader studying television genres and the reader interested in critical methodology.

Finally, a few words about the writing of this book may be of help. All chapters were written by Stuart Kaminsky with Jeffrey Mahan except for those chapters for which an author is indicated. All chapters were written expressly for this book and have appeared in no other publications. Special thanks are due to Charles Derry, Dennis Giles, and Marilyn Jackson-Beeck for their generous support in areas where the primary authors were less qualified to proceed.

Stuart M. Kaminsky

Jeffrey H. Mahan

part one

DEFINITIONS AND THE NATURE OF THE PROBLEM

—1—
A Historical Perspective on the Popular Arts

When we encounter any work of popular art, whether it is a nursery rhyme from near antiquity or television coverage of a baseball game, we are dealing with an apparent contradiction. The work of popular art is two things at the same time: it is like many other things that have preceded it; yet, it is also unique, not a precise duplication of anything that has been presented before. This leads to the basic debate about whether examination of works of popular art, or any art, should emphasize their familiarity of their uniqueness. Can a work be liked because it is both like other things and different from them at the same time?

For example, nursery rhyme songs often have the same melody although the words are different: the wordless structure remains the same; the verbal play varies. A child may delight in, or be indifferent to, the recognition that "Twinkle, Twinkle Little Star" has the same melody as the "ABC Song." The pattern of recognition for the child, indeed, is part of his or her own delight. There is a human need for recognition and repetition. Erik H. Erikson has pointed out in *Toys and Reason* that both the child and the adult need the stability of repetition as an emotional and aesthetic experience. Were a complete "uniqueness" possible, and it is not, it would remove stability, recognition, and, to a great extent, meaning for the individual having the aesthetic experience.

The antecedents of television drama, however, are difficult to identify. The history of our culture delineates the development of fine art and literature, but not that of popular art. It seems almost to have sprung full-blown ex nihilo. This is not, in fact, the case. The reason for this apparent lack of continuity can be found in an examination of our society's historical attitudes toward the arts.

From Rome to the Renaissance

In the "Masterpiece Theatre" series "I Claudius," there is an episode in which Claudius must deal with a maker of statues who has been commissioned to prepare decorative art for a party to be given by the Emperor Tiberius. The conversation takes a strong turn to irony when the artist forces the argument that his time schedule and payment are to be dealt with on the understanding that he is an *artist*, a person with special needs, talents, and considerations. Claudius has trouble with the argument, but he ultimately accepts the man's presentation of himself as more than a craftsman and is forced to deal with the inconvenience of doing business with a "special" person. Although it is not in fact the kind of conversation that would have made sense in ancient Rome, it reflects assumptions which would be quite common in twentieth-century England, where the series was produced. The idea of special status for the creator or his or her work is a relatively recent phenomenon. The Roman artisan would surely not have seen himself as a privileged creator.

A trip to the nearest museum housing artifacts of ancient cultures makes it quite clear that no apparent veneration existed for the creators. Their names do not even appear on their work. Until about the fourteenth century, Europeans did not separate the artist from other craftspeople. Art was a trade one learned. The artist would receive no more veneration for a statue than a bricklayer would for a wall, although he might well be better paid. The creative process—whether it resulted in functional art, such as religious paintings, or decorative art—was not considered either intellectual or particularly mystical. Art was a matter of training. There were people who could not be painters, just as there were people who could not make shoes, but one trade was not considered superior to the other. We need then ask, How did the assumption arise that artists are special and privileged persons?

Factors that alter long-standing cultural assumptions are often difficult to pinpoint, but the change in the status of some classes of creator from craftsmen to artists can be traced in European culture rather directly to events in the fourteenth century, particularly to the culture shock of the plague years. Had there been no plague, our attitude toward the act of creation, including our ultimate attitude toward television content in the twentieth century, would probably have been radically different.

The effect of the Roman Empire had been to create a nominally unified Europe in which trade and contacts among peoples were relatively easy. However, commerce and communication became much more localized after Rome fell and left European social structures in great disarray. The Roman Catholic Church did survive, however. The medieval empires that eventually arose in Western Europe relied heavily on the authority of the Church and strengthened it in turn. The Church became the keeper, not only of religion, but also of culture. Literacy was largely in the hands of the clergy; and it was in the church libraries that much of the old knowledge of philosophy, science, and history, as well as theology, was preserved.

During the plague years, even the preservers of culture shared in the common sense of siege by terrible forces from the "outside." The literature of the period is filled with images from the biblical Apocalypse—dragons, monsters, and armies from the East—all reflecting this great fear of encroachment.

In the face of this threat, the idea of the need for some sort of salvation increased in importance. People were dying in vast numbers from the plague, and so the living sought some form of transcendence. As keeper of the faith and preserver of art and literature, the Church was in a position to offer transcendence of two sorts: religious salvation, and an intellectual salvation that separated human beings from the animals, not because of persons' immortal souls, but on the basis of the mind. That is, human intellectual and creative faculties were seen as capable of rising to a plane that transcended mortality.

Thus, there developed an undercurrent of belief in a high art of the mind. Certain kinds of creation came to be seen as producing uniquely valuable art works which in turn could fully be appreciated only by those of cultivated mind. Some people began to think of themselves as aristocracy who alone could create, comprehend, and appreciate transcendent art. In fact, to a great extent the purpose of such high art was quite openly to differentiate such work—and its appreciators—from the merely common.

It must be remembered that it was the Church that was maintaining, and in many ways forming, the high culture. In fact, those who wanted to help create this culture had no place to find an audience outside the Church. For this reason, the high art of the period was aligned with religious concerns and ideas.

Popular art was seen as base and emotional. It was related to body responses—laughter, tears, and eroticism—which were suspect to the Church. On the other hand, high art concerned itself with matters of the soul. Its goal was to elevate the people from their base emotions and bodily needs and from the related popular songs and tales as well. High art, in contrast, emphasized the spiritual, along with reason and intellect. Obviously, this distinction confirmed some arts at the same time it demeaned the folk art of the masses.

Initially, these attitudes were quite reasonable responses promoting survival, since Europe was in turmoil, and civilization, "the culture," was definitely threatened. But the growing separation between the high and low arts had a variety of other consequences, which have affected intellectual life down to the present.

One effect, suggests Oxford historian Edward H. Carr in *What Is History?*, has been to distort our view of past civilizations. The songs, tales, cartoons, and dramas seen as low arts were regarded as at best meaningless—and usually as a source of embarrassment—by the clerics, nobles, and socially aspiring merchants who made up the high culture. Therefore the popular arts were seldom mentioned in the writings and records of the period. On the other hand, many paintings, poems, and histories of the high culture *have* come down to us. These evidences support the standard view of the age as one of great religious fervor. But it is important to remember that they were *selected* for preservation by the Church.

There was at the same time, Carr suggests, a vast pool of popular creative materials that had a wider audience than such religious images. The vast majority of medieval peasants shared an interest in folktales, erotic art, popular songs, and ballads about violence.

One way that these works were spread was by traveling performers. Ingmar Bergman's film *The Seventh Seal* depicts the medieval traveling two-person clown-and-stooge show, which continued into our day as the vaudeville-style two-person act. Often, these performances were staged quarrels or debates not unlike those of Abbott and Costello. Many of these forms developed a clown character who represented the aristocracy.

Printing and Protestantism

An important change in the spread of popular art took place in Europe at the end of the fifteenth century: movable type was invented. As a result, popular tales could be mass-produced. By 1500, presses had been set up in more than 250 European centers with forty thousand different books in circulation.

This development heightened cultural tension. There was a radical rise in literacy, for, with access to books, people had a reason to read. Many books were produced to sell as entertainment. In the period from 1500 to 1800, there were peddlers who carried bags of books to sell to literate folk. This growth of popular literature heightened the separation between the supposedly high and low cultures. The clergy and aristocrats, who had encouraged literacy, had not intended this. In fact, there was a certain amount of suppression of popular works, especially descriptions of murders and erotic art, both of which had a wide following.

It is difficult to know how widespread literacy was in this period. There are some church statistics, such as records of how many parishioners could write their names. Another indicator is how many books were being published and sold. Popular books, such as tales about highwaymen and other criminals, were sold at fairs and marketplaces. The amount of publishing that went on suggests a fairly high level of literacy. It is now thought that about 65 percent of the craft workers and some smaller percentage of the peasantry were literate.

As Protestantism arose in the 1500s, with its emphasis on each believer's searching the scriptures, literacy increased. In the Protestant states such as England, Scotland, and Sweden, literacy became very common well before the eighteenth century.

The question is, What were these people reading? The assumption has always been that they read religious tracts. They may have done that to a great extent, but there is another literature that is seldom acknowledged but needs to be dealt with. The literate aristocracy were committed to the elevation—to the religious and intellectual salvation—of the populace. However, at the same time, they held the distinct belief that the lower classes were not capable of very much; they could only go so far. The higher forms of culture and theology could only be grasped by the aristocracy or clergy.

Cultural Stereotyping Today

This kind of "doublethink" goes on in our own culture too. We are committed to getting the poor and uneducated to rise above their presumed criminal nature and devote themselves to religious or intellectual endeavors. At the same time, however, it's fairly evident that we still think they are animals, that they cannot become like "us." There is assumed to be a level beyond which such people cannot be trained. This attitude is part of our legacy and it affects a great deal of our thinking about popular culture in some very subtle ways. The function of education in the humanities was, and to a great extent still is, to perpetuate a high or elite culture. Teachers too often see their task as initiating students into the elite rather than to help the student explore and understand the various manifestations of our culture as it actually exists.

We are thus inheritors of attitudes developed in the Middle Ages. Our culture tends to carry on the assumption that the arts can simply and easily be divided into the high and the low. Educators have been taught to see their task as one of training their students away from low interests and developing in them an appreciation for high art. These assumptions are considered so self-evident in our culture that educators and critics feel no obligation to build a clear critical argument for their rejection of the low arts. The assertion that a detective story, comic book, or television show belongs among the low arts is regarded as sufficient ground to reject it and refuse to discuss it seriously as an art of creation.

The implications of these attitudes for the serious study of television are self-evident. Television is seen as lowbrow and vulgar. If it is discussed at all in the classroom, it is either to serve as a bad example of the common entertainments the educated person should learn to avoid, or to validate as high culture some rare example such as "M*A*S*H" or PBS's broadcasting of the BBC's "Tinker, Tailor, Soldier, Spy."

This book is based on a rejection of those attitudes about art and culture that encourage us to think of television as a wasteland of meaningless material that cannot be seriously engaged. Rather, we regard the medium as a shared cultural experience in which important questions are mythically addressed and social tensions resolved. In this it is like any other art form. Television will support serious critical reflection and discussion which will tell us about ourselves and the medium. The questions are, What will we ask? and, What methods of inquiry will we use?

—2—
What Is the Critical Task?

Television as Low Art

A major problem of television criticism and television teaching is that many, perhaps most, critic-teachers too frequently believe that it is their task to deal with values—to point out what is good so that it can be appreciated and to point out what is bad so it can be avoided. Rarely if ever do these critic-teachers establish some aesthetic basis for their pronouncements. Instead, these decisions are based on taste. The problems of aesthetics are difficult to deal with. Taste is relatively easy. We know, for example, that Shakespeare and Faulkner are "artists" and John D. MacDonald is a "hack." As critic-teachers, then, we can dismiss MacDonald or simply quote a line or two from his work and declare it obvious trash. By the same token, we can quote a line of Shakespeare and declare its beauty, depth, and insight. In neither case have we dealt with the substance of Shakespeare or of MacDonald and the detective story.

It is not difficult for a teacher to assert quality. His or her students are generally not confident enough to dispute such judgments. A critic can do the same. After all, the critic possesses the forum and has access to the medium of page or screen.

What has evolved is a criticism that has extended into the journals and the classroom, an imposition of contemporary taste as the touchstone of quality; the student is supposed to go armed to the television set and ask: Is the show about important issues? Is the creator sensitive? Are the performances good? Is the story morally acceptable?

Since the student is provided with the critic-teacher's predispositions and a recognizable milieu of taste, there is but one set of answers for popular television. All the answers come out in the negative.

The students then are faced with a decision. For perhaps twenty years or more, they may have responded to westerns, situation comedies, and horror tales and liked them; but they must now conclude that these are meaningless, trivial entertainment. They can join the history of taste and reject such works, or they can give up the pursuit of culture, proclaim that they have no taste, and continue to like popular television.

In such a situation the student is faced with relating his or her interest to the historically shared, class-biased assumption that art can easily be divided into high and low arts. Such a distinction assumes that the relative value of the art work is obvious and encourages the student to feel superior to popular television.

In turning from popular television, the student is then guided toward that which the elitist teacher-critic accepts and recognizes as "serious" television. So, though the student may have little interest in "art" television, he or she is readily convinced that the only good television shows are: (a) made by a handful of creators working in public television, (b) adaptations of acceptable art from other media, or (c) works from the "Golden Age" of television, and that one should be ashamed of liking popular television that may have seduced one's unwary mind.

By following such a pattern, television criticism and teaching have failed to meet a major responsibility. They have failed to help viewers and students find a meaningful way to deal with the vast majority of television content and its durability as a form of entertainment and to explain the fact that the overwhelming majority of people view, respond to, and return to situation comedy, science fiction, soap operas, Westerns, game shows, and cop tales as a source of ritual meaning.

The teacher-critic must have a way of responding to and understanding "The Jeffersons," "Dallas," "The Price Is Right," or "General Hospital." To do so is not to pander to popularity, but to recognize that popular television has serious validity.

Every popular television show can receive affirmative answers to the touchstone questions of quality mentioned earlier. Every show is about important issues. Indeed, one reason the viewer of a show is seeing the show is because it is a way of metaphorically dealing with the issues. For example, a private detective such as Thomas Magnum deals with our fears of loss of control in a complex society. Horror and science-fiction shows are surely operating at an important level about our fears of death and the future and our desire to understand or come to terms with these fears symbolically. As to the sensitivity of the creators, we must judge that ourselves through our response to the work. The word *sensitivity* is a loaded one, a vague and general term. It is of little value to consider creative sensitivity until we have some way of understanding what television shows are all about. Usually, if we like the work, we call it sensitive. If we do not, it is not.

The touchstone question of moral acceptability raises other problems. Moral positions change. A scandal of the Victorians is G-rated today. The critic or teacher's moral position may be drastically at odds with the moral position of the student and quite likely at odds with that of posterity.

The problem of taste that has affected television criticism is not unique to the criticism and teaching of television. It recurs in every area of aesthetics. As was discussed in the preceding chapter, this attitude has many of its roots in medieval times, when the Church attempted to sustain the "upper" classes through a literary tradition that differentiated them from the "animal-like" rabble. A split was discerned between mind and emotions; the mental course was seen as spiritual and superior, the emotional as inferior and animal. The two had to be kept separate. This legacy too often leads the critic-teacher to assume the role of the medieval priest: he or she attempts to raise students, or the public, to the "high art" of the mind, as it once was the task of the Church and its scholars to "raise" the populace from its base emotions. It is the totally conscious and supposedly intellectual artist dealing with personal images who is considered to merit attention and analysis. Popular works, being emotional and inferior, do not merit intellectual attention. "Low art," according to this argument, is simply entertainment, which is equivalent to a psychiatrist's saying a dream is just a dream.

Problems of Elitism

Universality and Individualism

There are a number of major flaws in the "high art" argument. First, the appeal of conscious creativity is grossly oversimplified. Supposedly, the psyche of the individual creator and his or her ability to use it creatively forms the chief subject of judgment. The more "individual" the work, according to this theory, the more artistic or creative it is, and, therefore, the more valid. Indeed, quite often, the more neurotic the work, the more attention it merits. Of course, this presupposes the ability of the critic-teacher to discern that which is individual and original—a rather fruitless task since every act of creation is related to other acts, traditions, or works. It is all too often one's lack of background in film, television, or literature that leads to the proclamation that what is in keeping with one's taste is unique or original.

For a television program to stay on the air, it must have broad appeal. Put another way the popular work can be examined on the basis of its being meaningful for a large group rather than meaningful for an individual. Perhaps the assumption to be made is that we share conceptions and problems, and the appeal or meaning of the work is inherent in our community as human beings. The traditional romantic approach has been that rare individuals create for themselves and that only those of us who are pure in heart—sensitive creatures—can be in tune with such artists and appreciate their work.

The Verdict of History

Another major flaw in the elitist argument is that history has shown that popular artists are quite often considered by posterity to be most creative. This has been so of poets, painters, novelists, and sculptors. The critics of the eighteenth and nineteenth century in all the arts were amazingly out of tune with our contemporary or even modern taste. Their lists of "great" creators of their own times are generally rejected now. Why should we assume that our elitist critic-teachers are different? If we do, we make an arrogant assumption to which every generation falls prey.

Obscurity and Accessibility

Another flawed assumption is that popular television is relatively easier to understand than "high art" and thus less meaningful and challenging to the intelligent individual. In truth, it is not harder to understand the plays of Shakespeare or the films of Ingmar Bergman, Luchino Visconti, or Michelangelo Antonioni than it is to deal with " Taxi" or "Charlies Angels." The traditional elitist way of dealing with "art" offers the critic-teacher a handle for discussing "fine" works. Such assumptions about accessibility are in fact a disservice, not only to the popular work, but to the "art" work as well. Complexity is not automatically a creative virtue; but even if it were, the Western or police tale can be quite as complex in execution, theme, and meaning as the "art" work.

The Middle-Class Tradition

A related problem is that most critic-teachers are not really capable of dealing with their own assumptions about high and low art. Polemically, for example, we might assert that, in the film study, the truly intellectual directors are generally shunned by the critic-teachers, not embraced by them. Such directors as Godard, Straub, Pasolini, Rossellini, and Antonioni are dismissed as obscure or confused because they are too difficult for the elitist critics-teachers of taste to deal with. Therefore, the elitist focuses on directors in the middle-class tradition, such as Bergman, Losey, Visconti, and Fellini. The critic-teacher also refrains from dealing with popular genre directors whose work requires a different context to be understood.

Type and Stereotype

The problems of the elitist critic-teacher are also founded on several assumptions about high and low art in the movies and television—assumptions that have become basic beliefs and that should be questioned. One assumption is that popular television stifles true art and reduces everything to stereotype for the masses. Because television shows are expensive to make, they must appeal to a large audience and therefore must be entertainment. However, the reduction to stereotype is not inherent in this process. It is true that popular television depends frequently on type, but immediately to use the pejorative term *stereotype* is to label that work inferior. Ulysses is a heroic type, and Falstaff is a comic type; yet we seldom hear either called a stereotype. Certainly, Dickens dealt in types. Clint Eastwood, James Stewart, and Robert Redford normally portray particular types, just as commedia dell'arte was based on fixed types. It seems there is a tendency to despise the economics of the medium and to call a type a stereotype if one wishes to debase it rather than deal with it.

Elitist critics also tend to fall back on the assertion that most popular television is bad but that there are certain works that transcend their type and limitations. This may well be so, but to come to this conclusion requires the articulation of an aesthetic, not the assertion of transcendence. In addition, the fact that a television show is a type, a genre work, even a formula work, is not automatically a condemnation. The popular work exists because of expectations. It might be argued that to transcend a type is to negate the type, to deny the continuing validity of the form. A genre (such as the western) does not exist simply to be negated.

Versatile and "Type" Actors

Another assumption of the elitist critic-teacher who disdains popular television is that one can also tell which shows are worth attention by who is in them. It is assumed that certain kinds of performance are superior to others. In truth, it appears that, in television, there are performers whom we wish to see perform. We wish to see them display versatility, not merge with their roles. Jack Klugman, Tony Randall, and Peter Falk are examples of such performers. For us to appreciate what they are doing, we must be aware of who they are.

Contrasted with performers are the "type" actors such as James Garner, Angie Dickinson, or Ron Howard. We assume that our concept of such a person as type will be exemplified in the roles they play. They are allowed some leeway by us, but we want—and expect—them to adhere to a type we accept and recognize. In many ways, this is difficult for the actor. The actor who can make it look as if he is not acting at all but is being himself has accomplished a great deal. To deny that this is difficult is to show a basic ignorance of how television shows are made—out of continuity, often in short takes, with dozens of people around, under difficult conditions.

One form of acting is not automatically superior to another. They are different and should be recognized as such. Certainly James Garner would make an incongruous Shylock, but Laurence Olivier would make an equally incongruous Jim Rockford.

Reality and Fantasy

A final elitist assumption revolves around the problem of reality. It has long been assumed that overt reality is creatively superior to fantasy or formula. We are back to the question of the psychiatrist and the dream. Our myths are embodied in our popular works, just as our problems with the mystery of existence are intertwined with the rituals and assumptions of religion. Indeed, it is possible that much popular entertainment functions as a replacement for religion as a source of myth. Our popular television shows are the ritual myths of large segments of society. They deal as much with the basic realities of existence as do documentary shows or naturalistic novels. Popular shows are concerned with our shared desire to explore through contemporary myth that which confuses and concerns us in the universe. "Barney Miller" deals comically, for example, with a very real human concern, the fear of urban existence and urban assaults on moral values. It does not matter whether we agree with the conclusions of the show; we should recognize and deal with the myths with which it deals and accept the validity of the material as worthy of creative effort. By the same token, the metaphor of spiritual possession in such series as "Star Trek" and "Outer Limits" for fears of loss of identity, fears of giving in to animal emotions and potential evils, expresses a basic psychological concern, a concern about something very real and enduring. "Masterpiece Theatre" is not automatically superior to these other shows because it expresses these concerns more overtly and with more conscious symbolism. Documentaries are not automatically superior because their level of symbolic reality is more directly related to history.

Genre and Aesthetics

Television aesthetics, like literary aesthetics, are tentative and inconclusive. In fact, when such aesthetics are tentative, they are of most value as potential areas of pursuit and testing. To turn a theory into a grid for testing television, however, results in the destruction of the theory when a show one likes falls outside the accepted boundaries. That is, a critic-teacher will distort an analysis of an appealing show to fit a theory he or she has accepted. Alternatively, the critic negates the show and bids it farewell because it does not fit the aesthetic. Thus, the theory of television becomes a sophistic tool that is actually used to impose taste.

The approaches to television explored in this book do not rest on taste assumptions or on theories of "high" and "low" art, but on the generic exploration of television. We believe any critical method should be based upon description and analysis, not the critic-teacher's taste. The question of quality can be left to the individual. The critic-teacher should function as a knowledgeable person who can help others understand what a work means and what it is doing. Prescriptive approaches are of only fleeting value.

3
Genre and Order

The word *genre* itself simply means order. All things are ordered by human beings so that they can be dealt with. To get through each day requires that we expect the world to behave much the way it did the day before. Each day is not a new experience to be relearned. Each event is encountered against a background of similar events and of expectations concerning the variables in each event. This is true of going to a gas station or turning on the TV evening news. The basic questions, however, are: What categories are there for ordering experience? How did they get there? What are the relationships among different categories? What do the categories mean?

In his book *The Order of Things,* philosopher Michel Foucault suggests that there are several basic ways of looking at order and that we must be aware of methods we have chosen. Each way of viewing order has its own basic assumptions, which we often believe others share when, in fact, they may not.

For example, according to Foucault, one way of examining order is based on the belief that order is inherent in all things, either as directed by a god or gods or through some "natural" order that evolved so that things can and do function. In other words, if you examine a frog or a comet or a television show, what you are doing is assuming that there is an order there for you to discover, an order which is singularly true. You are also assuming that, if you can discover this order, you can pluck it out and share it with others. At the most basic theological level, this sort of assumption has been a problem for several thousand years. If the order has been placed there, in frogs, comets, and television shows, by God or gods, how can we mere mortals ever discover the meaning of this order? But even beyond this problem, we have the assumption that there exists in all objects a basic truth that we can try to discover because it *is* there.

Kinds of Order

Up until the eighteenth century, the common assumption about order was theocentric. Astronomy, for example, assumed that the universe had to be ordered in a way that coincided with certain theological assumptions about the universe. Arthur Koestler's book *The Sleepwalkers* explores the elaborate and ingenious way in which European astronomers and physicists worked with the assumption that God put order in the universe and that the earth was the center of that universe. The seventeenth-century German astronomer Johannes Kepler, for example, evolved a most bizarre, beautiful vision of what the universe looked like because he assumed that everything must conform to a model with the earth at the center of a discoverable universe. When Kepler's contemporary Galileo said that the earth was not the center of the universe, he had to be challenged by the religious and scientific establishment, because he denied the common assumption about the basic order of the universe.

Assumption two is that there is no such thing as order; we really exist in chaos, and it is mad to think that any order exists. If, in fact, one believes in such an intellectual anarchy, there is really no sense in studying anything. If one believes that there are no associations, one cannot function in the world. You get up and you talk to people and you exist in a social-cultural situation, so you assume that everything is not chaos, that there is some sort of order and that things perpetuate. The assumption that there is no such thing as order, if taken seriously, would lead to a total inability to do anything.

According to Foucault, the third belief about order is that it is arbitrary. Relations perceived are created by the perceiver and may or may not be shared by others. They aren't necessarily clearly in the object. What you, as an individual, do is create order so that the world makes sense to you. You see three objects, and you want to make sense out of the three objects. What you do is try to see if there is a relationship among these three objects. And from your own background, you create and test potential relationships. In creating the relationships, you start altering your initial conception of what the order is in those objects. For example, when you see a group of people, you might say, "Ah, I see males and females, and I have certain conceptions about males and females." That is, you assume a generic order. But if you think about it, this approach is no more natural than any of a number of other ways of organizing our thoughts. What clothes are the people wearing? How do they relate in size, color, physiognomy? It is a matter of how you try to make sense out of what you encounter.

There is a recurring game on "Sesame Street" in which four objects or pictures are presented to a child, and the child is asked in song, "Which of these things is not like the others?" The objects might be three balls and a block or three children with umbrellas and coats and one in a bathing suit. The child on the show and the child at home are expected to discover the common cultural order which is assumed to be in the objects, to point out the object that does not fit in and thus to restore a proper order. Occasionally, however, a creative child will confound the assumption by seeing another order. For example, the child may say one of the three balls does not fit because the other two balls and the block have light colors and the ball he has pointed to is dark. Or the child may choose one of the people with the umbrella and coat as being unlike the others because the person he has chosen is a girl and the other people, including the one in the bathing suit, are boys.

What is at stake is how you deal with making sense out of the world. It is apparent that, according to this approach to order, the relationships we see may not be shared by others.

Foucault's fourth basic model of how one may view order is based on the beliefs that some perceptions are shared, and that genre and order exist as cultural truths. When we as individuals create a set of relationships, those sets of relationships may be sufficiently shared so that they will have meaning for other people. For example, when we say, "There is a game show on television this afternoon," we assume that we share enough experience about these words that others know what we are talking about.

Order as Cultural Consensus

There are certain cultural experiences human beings in a society share. There are also many experiences that we do not share. The ones that are not shared help to shape how we form a personal order and meaning. The ones that we do share shape how we as a society view meaning and cultural order. In this book we assume that there is a shared order, and we will explain this order and some of its potential meanings. The generic questions raised in the preceding paragraph would be: What do we mean by "game show"? How do we come to that terminology? And in what ways can we explore that? What do we expect of a "game show," and what does it mean to us?

We order things to make sense out of the phenomena of our experience and senses. Things happen to us. We are bombarded by experiences. We want to and must make sense out of these things, so we start putting them in an order. The order may be shared or may be individual. However, people are often considered insane when their own sense of order does not conform to a cultural norm. The insane person may employ unshared genres almost exclusively, having lost track of commonality and existing totally in a personal order. All too often, the perceivers of order are sure that their perception is correct, that there can be only one way of viewing the world. "I see it this way; therefore, there's no other way it can be." Political, social, and religious "isms" are based on the belief that there is but one proper assumption regarding how things are ordered and that anyone who sees order in any other way must be wrong.

Shared Perspectives and Television Programming

In subsequent chapters we do two things. The first is to decide what a particular show is doing that others are doing or have done and maybe what the similarities mean. The next question is, How is the show different from others and what do these differences mean? Those questions always have to be asked. They are part of the analysis of any individual work. How is it like other things, and how is it different from other things? Foucault's examinations in his books have been about science, medicine, criminology, and psychology. He believes that all these disciplines have been held back by faulty assumptions and sprung forward when these assumptions were questioned. For example, great misconceptions about anatomy were held for a long time because they provided an ordered way of looking at the subject. In fact, to question that order performing a dissection was a crime. The truth was known. There was no need to go further; and, besides, in going further, one might shake the accepted order and plunge the anatomical world back into chaos. It was essentially the same situation in astronomy. Major breakthroughs have often resulted when someone said, like the child on "Sesame Street," "I don't accept the order I've been taught to see. I want to put this thing in a context nobody has put it in before; I want to try another order."

Some people have suggested that the best way to study television content is simply to collect data, have people sit down with data banks, and put all the information into computers. The primary problem with that is that you first have to know what kind of questions you are going to ask and what kind of information you want to collect. When we realize that the questions in our minds are not necessarily universal questions but questions in which *we* are interested, it becomes necessary to identify them clearly before we proceed. When we look at episodes of "Cheers" or "The A Team," we have to have some questions in our minds first. We cannot just gather data. Information does not leap out of the television set in the form of basic truth.

Generally, when we talk about the idea of genre, we assume that the categories already exist and that we know what they are. A primary example is the western. We all think we know what a western is, based upon shared cultural understandings. But such assumptions have to be tested. What do we mean when we say "western"?

Another way of looking at generic order is to suggest that there may be ways of relating works that are not overtly connected by the culture but that tell us a great deal about one another when considered together. For example, *film noir* is a term created by two French critics who suggested after World War II that American movies could be looked at in a way that nobody had ever thought of looking at them. They made the suggestion and wrote a book and influenced many people, who said, "Yes, let's look at these movies in this particular way. They appear to be in different generic categories—some of them appear to be what people call Westerns; others appear to be detective stories; still others appear to be science fiction—but we can look at them in this different context, called film noir, which tells us something different about them."

One approach to genre study would be to look for emerging generic innovation. "The Dick Van Dyke Show," "The Mary Tyler Moore Show," and "Buffalo Bill" all present images of the television medium. We may now have enough examples to suggest a comic genre in which the media presents itself. The new form could then be explored to identify its plot conventions, settings, and character types.

It is important to realize that categories are not absolute or exclusive.

There is no reason why a particular show could not be tested or examined in several categories. If we could proceed logically to show a valid relationship among three, four, five, or six shows, even if nobody had ever thought about that relationship before, we would only be responsible for the logic of our position. We might, for example, have a category called "Violent Contemporary Presentation" or "Familial Interaction in Narrative Tragedies." Now, someone else may be talking about the cultural Western, and both of us may be using the same show. One of us is not necessarily wrong. We are using different categories to organize our experience of the show. It is strictly a matter of (*a*) whether we accept our basic assumptions, (*b*) how logical we are in terms of what we deal with, (*c*) how much sense our category makes, and (*d*) how our category helps us understand what we are talking about. We ultimately help each other by understanding the show ourselves in some context. So we have to find a context for that understanding.

Alternative Approaches

One thing, very simply, that we can do is to examine an individual television show in relation to a supposed continuum. In other words, we can say, "We want to look at 'Hill Street Blues' as a part of the continuation of tales about the police." If we want to go back to *Les Misérables* or to Greek mythology and see a continuum and can express the continuum, fine. How, then, does "Hill Street Blues" fit the continuum? In such an undertaking, the more limited the framework of our formula, the easier it is to handle.

One might look at similarities across generic or cultural lines. For instance, one of the authors of this book wrote a piece for *The Journal of Popular Film and Television* comparing Kung Fu movies and dance musicals. That was a created category, and it dealt with the relationship between two forms examined in terms of different kinds of performance. How are the fights in Bruce Lee movies like the dances in Fred Astaire movies? That is not a question most people are likely to raise in our culture; but, in raising it, we are providing various new ways of looking at the Kung Fu movies. What is going on in them, and why do certain things happen? They seem choreographed in a particular way. What might that choreography mean?

Another way to proceed, not quite as applicable to television as to film or other forms, is to deal with the idea of literary adaptation—

moving from one medium to another—and the meaning of that kind of generic move. In television, we can do it to some extent, but it is difficult. We might deal with a television series based upon a movie or upon a novel or play. We could do a comparison of the two, asking what the changes are from one form to another and what potential meanings there are in the changes. It would be interesting, for example, to compare the Norman Lear shows with their original versions from British television—compare "Sanford and Son" with "Steptoe and Son" and see what the differences and relationships are. Or Lear's "All in the Family" could be compared to "Till Death Do Us Part," its English original.

Another thing we could do is to cut across genres for period considerations. In other words, How do the television shows of a particular era compare? Is there some similarity among shows, regardless of their genres? Does anything peculiar in our perceptions characterize the early eighties, for example? Is such a peculiarity so pronounced that it becomes reasonable to organize the shows by period?

We could also take an authorship approach and explore the relationships between individual creators and genres. If we want to do this in television, it probably makes the most sense to do so in terms of the producer. And it should be a producer whose work has continued over a fairly long period in different forms so that one can see generic change. For instance, Garry Marshall produced "Happy Days," "The Odd Couple," "Mork and Mindy," "Laverne and Shirley," and "Joanie Loves Chachi." He also did made-for-TV movies and theatrical movies including *Young Doctors in Love*. One of the things that could be done is to gather this material—hundreds and hundreds of hours' worth—and try to see the relationships between Marshall as a producer/creator and evolution and change in the genres. The problem with such an approach is that it is very difficult to get this material, although reruns should make some of it available. A Norman Lear generic study related to comedy might also be possible.

There are, of course, other questions that could be pursued. One might explore the idea of heroism across generic lines. How do heroes function? What do they see as their responsibilities? How are they depicted? What values do they embody? What does the context define as affirmative or negative behavior? Some genres extoll virtues that other genres do not. Who are the antagonists, and how are they depicted? Often on television, what these characters look like is important. What do they represent? What do they say? Who are the bad guys in police tales, for instance? You will find that the bad guys in police dramas are nothing like the bad guys actual police officers deal with. Why is that, and what do the villains represent? What kinds of father figures, mother figures, career women appear in a particular genre? Who is chosen to portray these? What do they look like? Another thing to look at is what the endings are like. Is there some consistency to the endings in a particular form or a particular show?

Other elements we look at are more mythic. What are the problems set forth as narrative problems? What is raised as a problem for the protagonist(s)? Is there a group, and what is its composition? What are the settings like? What kind of information do we have about the setting? What kinds of things do we see? What kinds of locations are used? What tools do these people have? What kinds of jobs do they have? What kinds of people do they encounter? What are their jobs? What have they done in the meanings of their jobs?

However we decide to proceed, we have to lay out a method that explains and addresses questions we are asking of the text. Then we have to apply that method and ask those questions, of specific examples in which we are interested. Each time we do that, we clarify the generic order we see in a particular show.

4

The Differences in Media Experience

In a book about television genres, both terms are important: *television* and *genres*. The focus will be on the genres—what types of stories get told on television and what forms they take. These genres are not limited to the medium of television. A police tale or a comic romance might be found in a novel, on the stage, on radio, or on television. However, because of the unique form of each medium, the genre will be presented differently in each. Therefore, in discussing television genres, it is necessary to think about the unique characteristics of the various media. In this way, we will come to see what is unique about television as a medium and come to understand why an individual genre takes the form that it does on television.

The Novel

First, consider the novel. Many of its characteristics seem obvious and unimportant until they are juxtaposed with those of other media. For example, novels are almost always read by one person at a time. All of the input comes through the eye to the brain, which translates the print into words and then into images. This process is limited by physiology and skill. In order to be the right distance from the page and to control the pace, we read alone. Thus, by comparing the novel to other media, we see that one of its characteristics is the individual reader's control of the pace. The length of an individual work can be anything from fifteen thousand to two hundred thousand words, or perhaps longer or shorter than that. While the reader cannot control the number of words, he or she does control how quickly the information is absorbed.

Also, it is fairly clear that the amount of narrative information in a novel exceeds that of other forms. This does not mean you get more information in a novel, though a lot of people believe that. You get different information. Consider, for example, a film or a television series. In any individual image, there is a lot of data not immediately translated into words: the color of objects, the relationship of those colors to the characters within the image, how people move and gesture and who is going by, the objects in the frame, and the spatial relationship of people or objects to each other. In the novel there is more interiority—information about what characters are thinking and their emotional responses—simply because the written word allows for presenting thoughts in verbal form. This is difficult, though surely not impossible, in visual forms.

The Theater

A second medium is the theater. A very simple initial observation about it is that the play is performed for an audience sharing time and space with the production and performers. The size of the audience varies from a handful of people to thousands, and is limited only by the need to be in proximity to the stage. The ideal viewing location varies depending on the construction of the theater and perhaps the nature of the show. The question is, Where do you want to sit in relationship to the performance? A movement in modern theater, such as the Polish theater, has been to increase the involvement of the actors with the audience. While in the past actors had pretended to be unaware of the audience, now the interaction may be more direct. This may heighten our awareness of both the importance of an audience and the limitation of its size.

On television, and even more so in a movie, we are used to a constant change in the physical size of the characters. One moment, an actor is a tiny figure at the top of the image; the next, the bottom of his face fills the screen. In the theater, this does not happen. There may be a small change in our perspective as the actor moves upstage and down, but this remains negligible. In the theater, there is an actual space that the actors occupy, and our relationship to it remains constant.

Just as the theater space is not fragmented in the way that film space is, time is also constrained. Filmic devices that indicate passage forward or backward in time or the repetition of a single unit of time in different places are not readily available to the playwright. Time certainly may pass between acts and even scenes, but the assumption generally is that the performance time of any given scene matches the time of the events portrayed; if the dialogue takes ten minutes, then supposedly ten minutes have passed.

Though time-space limitations are greater in the theater, these very limitations of form may lead us to assume a greater realism. Because these are real people in an actual space, at the moment of our viewing, we may find what they say or do inherently more "believable." If so, this "realism" would be a realism of the form, that is, of the medium rather than the content.

As already noted, the reader controls the time allowed to absorb the narrative in a novel. Whether to absorb a few lines at a sitting with great care or to race through the book in a single sitting is up to the reader. Pace varies from perceiver to perceiver, and any reader may vary the pace from one text to another or even from one reading of a given text to another reading.

In the theater, it is the performers and director who control the time allowed for the narrative to unfold. In their preparation and in response to a particular audience, they can determine the pace. It is influenced by their sense of the play and the audience's response. They can change the performance depending on whether the audience is applauding, laughing, crying, sleeping, or talking. Like the novel, the play can be speeded up or slowed down, but in the theater, the viewer has little direct control over duration.

Film

With the emergence of film, the narrative pace became predetermined. Each viewing proceeds at exactly the same pace, and there can be no adjustment for a particular audience. If it takes fifty-eight minutes to see a particular feature, then every viewing will take fifty-eight minutes.

Radio

Radio introduced a further time constraint, the time slot. Radio also has the necessity of filling time with sound. Neither film nor television requires that. Radio established the split-decimal time periods that are so much a part of our American culture: thirty seconds, five minutes, fifteen minutes, thirty minutes, one hour. The whole system of commercial broadcasting is based upon the hour and the breaking up of the hour. Our minds are set up into patterns of listening to radio and watching television in terms of what an hour is and what the "proper" fragments of an hour are. Our primary time slots now in television are the half-hour, the hour, or the two-hour show. This is a totally arbitrary division based on the way our calendar has evolved and the breaking up of the days into hours. The broadcasting system is organized on the assumption that the length of the shows will be consistent. The radio show or the television program cannot be written to fill fifty-eight minutes one day, twelve minutes the next, and thirty-seven minutes the third. If it could, the TV schedule might look like this:

	Channel A		**Channel B**		**Channel C**
7:05	Farm News			7:12	Weather
7:17	Porky Pig	7:38	Morning Show	7:16	Bugs Bunny
8:11	Captain Kangaroo	8:43	The Gong Show	7:48	Days of Our Lives
	etc.		etc.		etc.

As the day progressed, the schedules would be further and further out of alignment.

This rationalization of time into quantifiable units beginning on the hour or half hour is not simply a part of the mass media. It is a part of the organization of Western society, which we have so internalized that we find it hard to imagine that, for most people in most periods of history, time was far more fluid. Festivals started when everyone was ready, and work lasted until it was done, whether that meant a six-hour or a twelve-hour day. This rationalization of time shapes the popular media in much the same way as it quantifies the rest of life. The workday lasts eight hours. Lunch lasts thirty or sixty minutes. The doctor can give you a quarter of an hour. Time has ceased to be a river and has become building blocks. If you doubt this, ask someone if he can give you seven minutes of his time.

The audience for radio, like that of television, is assumed. The listener is not present for the performance. The size of the audience varies greatly and is determined by the range of the transmitter, the number of receivers tuned into the station, and the number of people listening to each receiver.

With a movie, the situation is slightly different. Still, the audience is assumed; but they must gather in groups in specified places to see a film. A radio can be carried almost anywhere, but you have to go to a theater to see a movie; therefore, there are fewer sites for movies, but the audience at each is generally larger.

Television

Television is yet another matter. Like radio, it uses individually owned receivers. Because of the need to see the screen, the audience for any given receiver is usually small. Thus, though literally millions of people see the same programs, each viewer sees them alone or with only a few others.

Television shares with radio the rationalized time block based on the hour. Film has a greater freedom. Each tale can find its own appropriate length. But even here, there are conventions about what is the right length for a film. These have varied over the years. Currently, films are approaching a norm of about two hours, because most theaters show single features. There was a time when the assumption was that an "A" feature would run 77 to 90 minutes, while a "B" feature would be about 58 to 70 minutes long. One of the problems with showing films on television is fitting the film to the time block of 90 to 150 minutes. Often when the evening movie says "edited for television," the audience assumes that potentially offensive materials have been excised, when actually the cuts are to conform the film to the time slot.

One thing associated with television, particularly in the 1950s, was the assumption carried over from film that darkness was required for television viewing. It was assumed that television was like the movies. You turned the lights off, and you sat quietly, and you watched this phenomenon, usually on a very little screen. Because most people would not give over 20 percent of their house to turn into a theater, the reverence soon left. What happened as a social compromise is that the television set became part of the milieu of the total environment, people could wander in and out, talk, and break in. There was no reverence for the image. This has also affected the kinds of narrative and the information we get on television. Redundancy is often built into the television narrative by the people who create it, because they know there is a problem in the absorption of information while viewing. First, the viewer is not necessarily totally committed to watching. Second, he or she may be doing two or three things at the same time, with television viewing secondary among them. Third, the viewer is no longer sitting reverentially in a dark room, eyes riveted on the screen.

Today films, which used to have a quiet and respectful audience, are treated like television. The influence of television has, to some extent, affected a great deal of filmmaking. The ability to show "Battlestar Galactica," and more recently "The Day After," which were made as television shows, in theaters is an example of this change. At the most obvious level, the advent of television—especially the evolution to television in the late 1950s—resulted in audiences' talking more in movie theaters. Simply put, the reverence for the film image has declined. We may be seeing a slight shift back to a greater respect for the film theater as a place where one is quiet, partly because the cost of admission has increased and people are making a greater commitment when they do go to see a movie. Going to or choosing the film is often a social act and a significant expenditure in time and money. With television, you turn the set on, you make little commitment. You can turn it off.

Again, with film or television, the viewer has no control over narrative movement in time. One of the difficulties in studying radio, television, or film in its primary form is that it is difficult to stop the narrative. It is not like reading a book, where you can go back and read it more slowly. And if you want to see a show again, it is very difficult to do so, although the new videotape technology is making it easier. However, if the image is stopped or slowed down, it ceases to have narrative meaning; the technique becomes foregrounded instead of invisible, whereas you can read more slowly or more quickly and your brain will absorb it without necessarily becoming aware of the words or letters.

In other words, to a great extent, we control the novel—we control the written word. We have at least a semblance of control over the theatrical presentation, because we are dealing with human beings in a shared time and space. But we do not have that kind of control over electronic and mechanical media. They control us. That is not to say that television is an insidious thing; it is simply a recognition of our relationship to the medium.

Effects of Media Differences

What are the effects of these differences? We have already dealt with a few of them. To a great extent, the history of novels (or at least those novels affirmed as serious art) has indicated a reliance on the possibility of presenting thought processes. Introspection is primary, and the action of only secondary importance. That does not mean that there are not many novels that deal with action. But, when we start comparing the written word with other media, we find that the one thing that the written tale can do that the others cannot do as well is to present characters' thoughts. It is more difficult in theater, radio, television, and film to deal with what people are thinking. What is very cumbersome on television presents no difficulty at all in the written story. The mass media in general have not evolved narrative conventions for introspection as they have for action, dialogue, and proximity.

One of the things that the mass media do is to separate the performers from the audience. In the theater, the actors are there before us in space, and, when we applaud or hiss, we are communicating our responses to the performers and the performance. When we make the same response to a film, it is a different experience. It is nice when an audience spontaneously applauds a movie, but you have to ask whom they are applauding. Neither the actors, the director, nor the writers are present. When we applaud, we are not communicating our pleasure at their performance to them. For whom, then, is our applause? Unless we are applauding the projectionist for a particularly stunning job of projection, we must be applauding ourselves. It is what we think of as our own good taste that we are affirming. We, the audience, are the only people present, so that when we cheer, applaud, or boo, the film becomes an externalized example of our own taste. Applauding a play might say, "Yours was a marvelous and sensitive performance," to actors and perhaps an author who are actually present. With a film, the applause must say, "We are a marvelously sensitive audience able to appreciate the richness laid before us."

One of the authors attended a performance of *The Brig* in a tiny theater in New York. It was a small crowd on a weekday night after the play had been running for many months. At the end, a little old man got up and called for the author. The chance of the writer of the play being in the audience on this weekday night when nobody was there and the play had been running for months and months was nil; but it was part of his assumption that being in the theater he had a relationship to real people, and therefore the author would be there and would come out. It is an interesting idea that in the theater you are dealing with real people and they are there; but when you are dealing with radio, television, or film, you are not dealing with real people.

Media Conventions Compared

Convention becomes crucial in all media. The conventions of theater are extremely rigid. We must enter into and "believe" the story that is being performed at the same time that we appreciate the performance of real people who are actors performing the story. We know they are human beings who can make mistakes—they can fall down; you can interrupt them or give them some difficulty; all sorts of things can happen to them—but they are engaged in a performance, and we are attending a performance. We are pretending that, while they are up there performing, we think that they are really in a room in England in 1872 or in New York in 1927. It is an enormous part of the convention of watching a play that we ignore many of the things we see. We ignore that we see the edges of the theater and that there are people sitting in front of us. We ignore the fact that, when people perform in a normal-sized commercial theater, they are shouting. They have to project in order to be heard. We have learned to accept the convention of projection as something different from shouting. Our minds tell us that they are not shouting, that they are talking normally; but they are not talking normally. It is a convention we accept.

These conventions prevail in other forms. In radio, we have very rigid verbal, musical, and sound conventions. There is a definite "art" of sound convention in radio. An important convention in narrative radio is that of talking to oneself, which we carried over to some degree in early television. As he walks into a room, someone will say, "I had better be careful or I'm going to run into that chair. I'd better get out of the way; who's that coming down the. . . ?" Even a contemporary listener will accept this device as part of radio convention.

We accept the presence of a narrator on radio, someone who fills in the gaps in the story line for us. The narrator is also conventionally acceptable in documentary film. But The Voice has gone out of style on television and in narrative film to the point that a narrator is now sometimes used to create a nostalgic feel. For instance, on the show "Kolchak: The Night Stalker," Kolchak narrated his own tale. In the Sherlock Holmes radio series, Dr. Watson would talk to the announcer of the show, tell him the story. The announcer would comment, "What story do you have for us today, Dr. Watson?" Dr. Watson would reply, "I'll tell you about the time Sherlock Holmes and I did. . . ." This would be followed by a break, and the announcer would say, "Now let me tell the people about Bromo Quinine Cold Tablets." After the commercial, the announcer would say, "Now, Dr. Watson, get back to the story." Sam Spade on the radio was talking to a dictaphone, like Kolchak to his tape recorder. The Lone Ranger was constantly talking to himself to make it clear what was happening. The running monologue was a convention that the audience was urged to accept.

From this it could be suggested that radio is a writer's medium. If the play is the performer's medium, to a great extent, radio is shaped by the writer.

Radio, even live radio, moves away from the idea of theatrical performance—you are not with those people; you do not have to worry about how they feel or that they are going to be upset if you do not applaud. The electronic media provide a distance.

In television, conventions of format or formula are very important. The heavy emphasis on formula reflects the nature of television as a medium. Television relies heavily on recognition of character types and of the formats, partly because along with radio it appears in your house as free entertainment and thus extracts a minimal commitment on your part. There is a very heavy emphasis on genres in narrative television; and the little bit of remaining narrative radio also relies on formulas or genres. Recognition is extremely important. We see a Western, a romance, or a cop show, and we know what it is and how it can be categorized; and the networks categorize shows this way. There is only so much attention that the home audience will give to narrative information. Television shows, whether consciously or unconsciously, are created in recognition of that. The shows are written in a kind of shorthand which requires, to a great extent, that the audience understand the cultural context in which the information is given. The assumption is that the audience recognizes certain types and patterns and appreciates the repetition of these story patterns, myths, and character types that constantly recur.

In television, it is producers who are the primary creators. They have more control than actors or writers. In fact, writers very often become producers; it is a primary way of moving up in television.

In radio, there was never a great reason for writers to become something else; the best thing to be was a writer. They had the greatest control of the medium.

In film it is different. Supposedly one moves up to being a director. Because films are not usually made in extended series, control of an individual film is important. Thus, the director of an individual film is affirmed, whereas, on television, it is the producer who controls the series, perhaps using a different director each week. For that reason, film is often considered a director's medium.

Furthermore, film, to a great extent, is larger than life—and not just metaphorically; it is literally larger than life. When one goes to the movies one sees figures who are bigger than real people and this is essentially different from all the other media. In a film closeup of an actor, depending on the size of the screen, a fifty-foot-tall head is possible. This may relate to the idea of the movie theater as a popular culture cathedral. Actors are seen in our history as being bigger than life. The kind of celebrity status people achieved in film has, at times, been quite different from the status of television actors. Film actors are seen as being bigger than life and not like other people, whereas, in television, an actor is assumed to be a person like the rest of us, who was lucky enough to have made it.

People often say that, in films, there is more time to develop what can be said, because a film can be seventy, eighty, or ninety minutes, or two hours long. When we compare individual films with television *series*, however, the time factor changes. The television series, even in the course of one season, is much longer than an individual film. What is different is that in a television series there is segmentation. The ongoing narrative is fitted to the half-hour or one-hour slot.

In the continuing television narrative, there is a series of narrative units, little segments in which the narrative action takes place. Those units are tied together. The relationships between the characters are ongoing, so that, even if there is dramatic resolution in each segment, the audience has a sense of a continuing story. The relationships may change with the narrative progression, particularly over several seasons. An example would be the change in the Major Houlihan character on M*A*S*H. She began as the "Hot Lips" character from Robert Altman's movie, the constant butt of sexual jokes; but, over the years that M*A*S*H was on television, she came to be a sympathetic character, presented as a professional member of the medical team. Corporal Klinger made a similar progression, as he took over the dramatic function that had previously been fulfilled by Radar O'Reilly.

In the miniseries, or the multi-episode segment of a regular series, the dramatic progression is carried on with the same sort of "hook" that was used in the old movie serials. Some question is left unanswered at the end of each narrative unit. The conventions are such that we assume the question will be answered in the next unit. If we have been "hooked" by the question, we will attempt to see that next unit. Each installment in a series is further subdivided in this way to make room for commercials. The commercial interruption comes at a particular time, and the narrative presents a hook, just before breaking away, to bring us back after the break.

Often, a miniseries will be based on a novel. When the tale moves from the print medium to television, one of the tasks of the screenwriters will be to break it up into narrative units. If it will run for five nights, then the screenwriters must create five narrative units, the last one usually being obvious, because it is the end of the novel. But then they have to find four others and create for each a temporary conclusion—temporary because it leaves some questions unanswered. In order to get the viewer to watch the next time, the screenwriters have to raise questions so that people want the answers. This follows the narrative pattern of the soap opera.

For years, before television, it was normally accepted that one could walk into a movie at any time and then see the movie again and pick up the story. With the advent of television, that changed to the point where now it isn't an accepted practice. That may be because of the experience with television. In television there aren't immediate reruns. If one misses the beginning, one cannot see it immediately after the conclusion, so the habit of picking up narratives in the middle and piecing them together has been abandoned.

Television presents genres that we know from other media, but they are presented in a unique way. Television narratives are characterized by the use of rigid time categories and the repetition of information in a variety of ways to reach an audience that may not be giving the story full attention.

part two

HISTORICAL AND STRUCTURAL APPROACHES

Every new television show or series is part of a continuum, the result of a history of trial and error and an attempt to vary a formula in the hope that the variation will touch a massive audience. So, as we indicated earlier, each show is both formulaic and original at the same time. The critic can do one of two things about this apparent contradiction. (1) He or she can explore the similarities, try to discern the structure that has evolved. By *structure*, we mean the broader elements, such as plot, and the more specific elements, including motifs and characters. Once this structure has been traced to determine *how* it has evolved, an attempt can be made to consider *why* it has evolved—what meaning or meanings that structure has and why it is manifest in this particular form. (2) The critic can also concentrate on the specific show or series, try to determine what is different about it, how it varies from the conventional structure, and what that variation might mean. The danger in this concentration on the original is that the originality cannot be determined unless one knows the history of the form. How, indeed, can we know if something is a variation if we do not know what the tradition is from which it varies? This is one reason why so many critics who profess to dislike television have so much trouble understanding a particular show and coping with its relationship to the history of the medium and, indeed, the history of popular art.

French film critic André Bazin, when he was editing the influential film magazine *Cahiers du Cinéma*, said, "Let him who likes it write about it." The supposition was that the critic who liked the work, the genre, the formula, would be more likely to know its history and structure, to appreciate and respond to it so that others who shared his or her response would most profit from that criticism.

To write about quiz shows, police tales, or soap opera in a historical or structural context requires a knowledge of these genres, a willingness to ask questions, and an interest in extensive listening, watching, and responding. The initial step is to be moved or entertained by the form and to enjoy the pursuit of its evolution or structure, which is meant to be the case in the next four chapters.

In chapter 5, which deals with quiz and game shows, the attempt is made to apply a structural approach, created by literary critic Northrop Frye, to a non-narrative form. One reason for doing so is to try to extend critical methods of literary analysis to popular works and discover if such methods provide some understanding of entertainments which lack narrative form.

In chapter 6, a historical perspective is given to the police tale and an attempt is made to chronicle briefly its evolution in the media and, in so doing, establish its importance to the viewer as contemporary myth. This, in fact, ties in to the chapter on quiz shows and game shows because it suggests that the mythical pattern is one that can be traced historically and that the tracing itself, while not an answer to the meaning of the form or the variation, is needed if an analysis based on knowledge and not prejudice is to be made.

In chapter 7, Dennis Giles takes another structural approach, that of the Russian formalist Vladimir Propp, and applies it to the police tale. Propp's original work was designed to explore the structures of Russian fairy tales. Giles takes Propp's discovery of a reasonable structure and explores its applicability to the police tale, discovering that Propp's structure can tell us as much about the order of a popular narrative as it can about a particular ethnic formula.

The chapter on quiz shows applies a structure created by Frye to understand one formula; the chapter by Giles does the same thing with Propp's created structure. At this point, it is essential to emphasize that any of the applications or approaches made in this section can be applied to any formula. If the approach is a worthwhile one, there is no mystical reason why it should explain only one genre and not another. The telling point is that the person who chooses to apply a particular method has done so because of an interest in both the method and the formula or genre. This entire section could be a series of applications of Frye, Propp, or other structural critics to a great number of genres or individual shows. However, the goal is not to exhaust possibilities but to introduce approaches and the very idea of structural criticism.

It is common for the author of a book or a teacher to be approached by someone who asks why that author or teacher didn't talk about a particular show or event. The reasonable reply is that it is impossible to satisfy everyone's individual taste and interest. Not only is it impossible, it is unreasonable and not particularly productive even to try. What is productive is to suggest ways of approaching individual works or genres, structures to be applied so that the person who asks the question can take that approach and engage in his or her own application. Critics or teachers can choose the examples that they wish. You, as reader or audience, must choose your own examples and/or interests.

In chapter 8, based on his extensive viewing of daytime drama, Charles Derry creates a structure to help explain the soap opera formula. In fact, as he suggests, the very idea of seeking a structure leads to an understanding of possible meaning.

The dismissal of some element or character as stereotyped or the soap opera as formula is, as Derry points out, a failure to understand the continuing importance of such characters or formula. We are back to the idea of difference and similarity. Derry, to a great extent, is arguing the case for mythic meaning, the desire on the part of the audience to seek repetition, which is clearly akin both to the child who delights in hearing the same fairy tale over and over again and to the educated adult who, in spite of the thousands upon thousands of supposedly fine works of fiction in the world, will reread a particular work by a favorite author. The child will simply say that he or she likes Goldilocks. The adult will rationalize that *Ulysses* is singularly great, that the decision is not personal but objective, in spite of the fact that few people share his or her extreme commitment to that particular work.

Quiz shows, police tales, and soap operas have something very important in common. They have all been considered essentially meaningless, acts of arid entertainment without form and substance. The articles in this section argue that they have both form and substance and that the proof of the value of the work is not necessarily in the work itself but in what we as individuals and critics choose to make of it.

—5—

An Application of Northrop Frye's Analytical Methods to Quiz and Game Shows

For any critical effort, a method or model is necessary to organize the material if the criticism is to be used by others besides the critic. Ideas that Northrop Frye developed in *Anatomy of Criticism* will be used here to discuss quiz and game shows.

Drawing on Aristotle's *Poetics*, Frye suggests that tales can be classified "by the hero's power of action, which may be greater than ours, less, or roughly the same." By treating the participants on a game show as analogous to the protagonists in a story, Frye's categories can be used to organize and type the game shows and discuss what they might mean.

Where the protagonist's power is greater than ours, Frye calls the protagonist a *god*. Where it is less than ours, he calls the protagonist a *fool*. Frye has two categories to identify protagonists who are roughly analogous in power to us: they are *heroes* or *men*. Thus, the game show can be discussed by asking if it involves contestants whose power is greater than the audience's (gods), roughly equivalent to the audience's (heroes and persons), or less than that of the audience's (fools).

Protagonists as Gods

Hierarchically at the top are shows in which gods are tested—not literal gods, of course, but superior cultural beings who can be seen metaphorically as gods. In such shows, we find celebrity experts as panelists. They are presented to be admired for their knowledge. Shows in this category tend to be glorifications of the idea of knowledge, or of special education. They reflect the belief that all questions have answers. This kind of show is not currently very popular. In fact, we have no television series at present in this category. The English radio shows "My Word" and "My Music," which appeared on a few U.S. educational stations, do fit this category. In such shows, the audience does not know the answer to the questions. The people on the panel are supposedly superior to us, because they have special knowledge; they are "intellectual heroes," but their mythic function is different from that of the hero. They are, in one sense, data-ists. In Frye's hierarchy, they are better than human and thus superior to the audience, because they possess the knowledge our culture most treasures: data. They are humans who can function as data-retrieval banks, computers with a sense of humor. One might argue that with real computers available, such humans are not needed as popular culture gods.

In radio, the most popular example of the god category was "Information, Please," which lasted from 1938 through 1952. The prizes given away were encyclopedias, books that symbolized or represented data or information. If you could stump the panel, then you were worthy of owning an encyclopedia. Participants were designated by their special knowledge and superior intellects. People would send in letters asking questions that were supposed to be very difficult, questions not of opinion or judgment but of data. A typical and actual question used on the show was: "Can you name five operas in which a witch is murdered?" "Information, Please" was the most popular of this kind of show, and it went briefly into television. Another "gods" show on radio was "Noah Webster Says," in which people had to give definitions from the dictionary without going to the dictionary. You would send in a word, and the panelists had to define the word and talk about its origin.

On television, Chicago was the center for the gods show in the fifties. "Down You Go," hosted by Bergen Evans from Northwestern University, was a principal example which involved asking supposedly intellectual questions of a panel of experts. Evans quickly became the resident intellectual for television and gained fame as the person who verified the questions for the "$64,000 Question": "These questions have been checked and verified by Dr. Bergen Evans from Northwestern University." Remember, it does not matter if we really think these people are actually superior. The programs present them as being superior.

John Daley, who hosted "What's My Line?," also hosted "It's News to Me," with experts on people in the news, details about the news, and specific data about the news. Another show, "Who Said That?," often had governmental figures, senators, who could identify quotations that other people could not.

Protagonists as Heroes

The next category, moving down from top to bottom, is that of celebrities as heroes. In the first category were the intellectual celebrities, people identified as Professor or Senator, who had superior knowledge. In the second category are celebrities as heroes but not gods. They are likely to be well-known entertainers who do not necessarily have more knowledge than anyone watching. What they do have is superior poise. They have the ability to perform and make jokes under pressure. "What's My Line?" is an example of such a show. Other examples are "I've Got a Secret," which started in 1952 with Garry Moore as the host, and "To Tell the Truth," which began in 1950. The implication in such shows is that panelists are slightly superior to the viewer, but only in their ability to perform under pressure, which is, essentially, the challenge to any mythic hero. "Hollywood Squares" is a very good example. In radio, the heroic quiz formula wasn't popular. Perhaps it may have had something to do with the fact that the audience could not see the celebrity performers. The television show that lasted the longest in this category was "What's My Line?," which began in 1950 and kept going well into the 1970s.

Perhaps because the shows used celebrities as panelists, the programs in the first two categories gave away no money to the god or hero participants. Prizes and rewards go only to those who defeat the gods or are aided by the heroes ("Password," "Hollywood Squares," "I've Got a Secret," etc.).

Another form of the hero game show involves noncelebrities who claim to possess special knowledge. The gods had some socially acceptable sign of their superiority such as a degree or a professorship or book authorship. These noncelebrity heroes aspired to do what the gods or heroes did but lacked the mythic protection the gods had. They acted out of hubris, excessive pride or vanity, which arises when a mortal challenges the gods. They may fail and be punished for their audacity; but, because the mythic dangers are great, the rewards are correspondingly great. It is in these shows that we begin to find big money prizes.

An example of the noncelebrity hero show would be the "$64,000 Question." It was among these shows that the quiz show scandals of the 1960s took place. It is likely that nobody would care if celebrity shows were fixed. On "Hollywood Squares" there is, in fact, an announcement that the contestants are provided some answers in advance. But with hero shows, the assumption is that we are watching a metaphorically real challenge, and the enormity of finding out that it was a fake was an affront to our mythic feeling. That is why the scandals were treated so seriously. It was not just the amount of money. What made an even greater difference to us was the fact that we found out that the metaphor we thought we were watching did not have any substance. Therefore, the person who had lied about challenging the gods suffered enormously and had to perform an act of public contrition.

For various reasons, nothing like this existed on radio. If we go back and listen to radio quiz shows, we find that very little money was given out. During World War II, if a serviceman happened to be on a quiz show and answered the $64 question, the host would occasionally double the money at the end and he would get $128, but nothing enormous.

"Dotto," a connect-the-dots game, involved large amounts of money. Dotto was the show that led to the breaking of the quiz show scandals, but it did not involve as much money as some of the others, and the other shows got more publicity. The "$64,000 Question," hosted by Hal March, had its heyday about 1955. It spawned a second show called the "$64,000 Challenge." But even these were not the top money givers on television. The largest prize on television was awarded by the "$100,000 Surprise" hosted by Mike Wallace.

Three shows were involved in the scandals: "Dotto," "$64,000 Question," and "21," hosted by Jack Barry, on which the "fix" was announced. The accusation was that the producers were "feeding" answers to contestants to make the show more suspenseful and create a narrative; the illusion of challenging the gods was broken. In fact, the gods of the networks were controlling the supposed heroes. Prometheus was a sham, and the public wanted public execution. Contestant Charles Van Doren became the scapegoat and made a tearful televised apology.

Protagonist as Poised Common Person

The third category, that of noncelebrity participants whose knowledge doesn't exceed ours but whose poise must exceed ours, now is a very important form on television. In this form, we find the supposedly common person who has more poise than the average but doesn't display any great knowledge. Important, however, are grace under pressure and quickness of response. Sometimes, this ability is tied to an assumption of physical skill and the person's need for the money. That which protects participants in their challenge to ordinariness is their need for money. If their need is great, they can display some superiority and we can still cheer for them. The possibility of their making money is there, but not the enormous amount of money evident in some of the other categories. In this category, work is involved, not just answering questions but doing something: pressing the button faster than somebody else, or some other token of work. Actual work was involved in some other shows such as "Beat the Clock" with Bud Collier. A clock was set, and the contestants were given a challenge, something they had to do. If they could do the work faster than other people, they would make money. Dick Clark's "The Krypton Factor" is clearly in this category. A show like the "$10,000 Pyramid" is related to this idea. The work is not as physical, but it involves quickness and how fast the contestant can respond. "Family Feud" is based, not only on speed, but also on the ability of the person to demonstrate his own connection to the norm. Contestants are rewarded for being able to guess what a group of supposedly random people believes.

Protagonists as Fools

In the category of fools, those below the viewer, we find the noncelebrity whose knowledge doesn't exceed ours and who is less poised. We are encouraged to feel superior to these participants, who are often punished and only minimally rewarded for their willingness to be punished. They choose to be fools. They participate in the game with the understanding that they are going to be humiliated. For the reward of temporary social recognition, they willingly play the fool. Some of the most popular shows on radio and television are about people who are willing to do this. "Truth or Consequences" was the longest running show in this category. "The Gong Show" also followed this pattern. The "$1.98 Beauty Contest" presented itself as being an impromptu talent show but was rehearsed—the people knew in advance the degree of their humiliation.

"Truth or Consequences" was enormously popular. There is even a town named Truth or Consequences in New Mexico. On the show, contestants answered a question, and, if they got the right answer, they were given a little tiny gift and bade farewell. But almost nobody got the right answer. They were not supposed to get the right answer. The point was willingly to pay the consequences, to suffer comically. The consequences almost always involved making a fool of the participant, for which he was then given some token gift such as a Travelaid suitcase from American Airlines. "Truth or Consequences" was created by Ralph Edwards on the radio, and then it moved to television where Bob Barker hosted it.

Another example of a fool show was "Almost Anything Goes," hosted by Soupy Sales, in which teams from different towns competed against each other in contests involving swimming in whipped cream or putting bananas in their ears. For such antics, they received a small trophy.

A variation of the fool show involves those who are ridiculed but are well rewarded for their willingness to be ridiculed. One takes some sort of punishment, abuse, or ridicule but is rewarded for it. In short, the humiliation is not its own reward. "Supermarket Sweepstakes" was one such show. "Let's Make a Deal" has evolved into such a show because the people who participate think that is what it is. They act as if they have to dress up and make fools of themselves. But they did not originally have to. The producers never said, "If you want to be on the show, make a fool of yourself and dress silly." People thought it was that kind of show, so they started to dress up like chickens, spacemen, or boxes of cereal. When people started to assume that was what this show was, the producers accepted it and incorporated it into the show.

Another variation, in which the contestants are rewarded for letting the audience feel superior to them, is the confessional show. The

Richard Dawson moderating "Masquerade Party" during the 1974-1975 revival of the show.

participant makes a public confession and then is rewarded for the confession. There were a number of these on television in the 1950s. "Queen for a Day" is a very good example. People were rewarded for telling how miserable their lives were. If you had a more miserable life than the other two people on the show, you became Queen for a Day. You deserved a reward for the misery of your rotten life and for going on television or radio and telling what a miserable life you had. You won by proving how low you were, how superior the audience was. The fool's misery or punishment confirms the superiority of the audience.

An extreme example of this format on television was "Strike It Rich." Participants did not have to answer any questions. All they had to do was tell how miserable they were. There was a phone on the stage, and that phone was open for anybody to call who wanted to help. The contestants' task was to come out looking as pathetic as they could, with their family, little kids, aunts, uncles, grandfathers, all wearing raggedy clothes. Then the "Heartline" would ring. The call might well be some industrialist in the suburbs of Cleveland who said, "I'll give these people a job and $4,000." The contestants' responsibility and role were then to break down and cry, with the audience applauding. "Strike It Rich" didn't give money. Someone from the outside gave money. People were being rewarded for proving to the viewers that they were better off than the contestants.

The hierarchy, according to Frye's categories, is relatively clear: from shows in which the superior participants did not need financial reward for participation to those shows in which individuals needed to do nothing other than demonstrate their financial need.

Do we simply watch these shows because we like game shows and quiz shows, or do they represent some sort of image of how we want to view the world for at least that period of time?

It is important to note that no single method of analysis explains everything about a given game. Different approaches will highlight different facets of the genre or formula under consideration. For instance, the old radio and television series "The Quiz Kids" could be fitted into Frye's model as a somewhat unusual example of the gods category. However, one might propose an alternate structure that would raise more interesting questions than Frye's does about that show and its relationship to the audience.

Shows as a Means of Resolution of Social Conflict

One way to proceed would be to suggest a category of shows that present the temporary resolution of social conflict. Instead of asking if the participants are superior, equal, or inferior to ourselves, we would note that these shows pit one group which represents something against another which represents something else. What people seldom remember about "The Quiz Kids" was that the quiz kids were really competing with the adults who sent in the questions. If the adults stumped the kids, the adults got the money. They could get questions from anywhere in the world, and the kids, who had a godlike, superior knowledge, tried to answer them. It is easy to suggest that mythically the show was about generational conflict. In fact, there were instances in "The Quiz Kids" in which they literally competed with their own parents.

One result of the television show "The Quiz Kids" was an almost morbid media interest in what happened to the kids later. Nobody cared about the people in the other categories (except, perhaps, for the "$64,000 Question"). For years, there was a continuing interest in the problems the quiz kids had later in their lives. A kid who acts like a god is performing a dangerous act of hubris which we expect will lead to punishment.

The audience's averageness is affirmed by the suggestion that exceptional people, particularly children who exceed the limitations of their parents, suffer for their excesses. By finding four or five former quiz kids who suffered later in life, the news media could glorify the myth by saying, "Look, see what happened to them? Being so smart was a challenge to the gods, and they have paid the price."

Variations on the quiz kids were radio shows called "Are You a Genius?" and "Youth Versus Age," with children competing against adults. While youth versus age is a conflict in which we have been particularly interested, Western myth and culture could suggest others. The film *The Longest Yard* was based on the premise that the prison football game represented the conflict between prisoners and guards. One could also ask whether quiz and game shows until "Family Feud" have attempted to avoid contrasting groups of black and white contestants so as to keep the shows from representing racial competition.

On television, there have been a few extreme examples of competition. One show which did not last very long was called "Brains Versus Brawn." The idea was that people who were smart would compete against people who were strong, but the producers didn't know quite how to formulate the competition.

Shows That Deal with Life Anxieties

Another approach to structural meaning in quiz and game shows might be to ask, not about conflict between social groups, but about conflict with fate. Do shows that involve gambling attempt to resolve the anxiety about the arbitrariness of much of life? On many contemporary shows, we can make a choice to go on or not to go on. The gambling element has increasingly become part of the format. Chance takes the place of skill, so that what is at issue is the willingness of the participants to gamble. In these shows, the viewer often engages in watching a narrative progression that suggests that the participant is determining her or his own fate. We do not know what the answer is going to be or whether the gamble is going to pay off. "Let's Make a Deal" is the primary example.

These shows tend toward romantic resolution. They present a world in which most people win. In our lives, perhaps, most people do not win, but built into these shows is a high likelihood that one who takes a chance will win. "The Price Is Right" has some of this element. Radio had a lot of these shows, like "Break the Bank," "Take It or Leave It," and "Double or Nothing." On the "$64,000 Question," one could always stop at any point, but few did.

In all of these shows, whatever their category, there was and is an attempt to convert a disordered world into a means of triumph over chance, either through a physical willingness and ability or through mental retention. Intellect rarely seems to be very important. In spite of the shows' surface-level claims about the importance of intelligence, other qualities are more important in the struggle to triumph over the adversities of fate as they are enacted in the quiz and game shows. A good memory, quick reaction under pressure, or physical abilities are more likely than exceptional intelligence to lead to triumph. That is powerful mythology.

In all this, we come to see that, like narrative television, the quiz and game shows have their own conventions that can be explored. And those conventions vary, depending on the kind of basic cultural conflict the show attempts to resolve. Thus, as we find methodologies such as Frye's which allow us to discover the underlying questions these shows answer for us, we begin to understand, not only what we like, but why we like it.

—6—
The History and Conventions of the Police Tale

One way to begin to study a genre is to catalog its conventions. What things have become the normative elements of the formula? How is the genre like and unlike other similar forms? What sort of protagonist appears in these tales? Where do they take place? With what sort of people does the protagonist come in contact? What objects have meaning within the tale? How do the stories typically unfold? Answering these questions can help us to understand what is unique about a formula and how a particular example fits into the genre. What follows is an attempt to raise these questions about television police tales.

History of the Police Genre

Police tales are often categorized with the tales about private detectives, criminals, and spies. However, it seems fruitful to deal separately with those that take as their protagonist one who is vocationally identified as a police officer. Unlike other popular forms, these tales have a relatively brief history, with roots in the nineteenth century. To a great extent, the police did not exist as a separate profession until the last century. Those who apprehended criminals before this time were soldiers, as they still are in Italy and some other countries, or extensions of the judicial system, as in contemporary Soviet Russia. In England, a police force began when the judges started to pay people—usually "reformed" criminals—out of their own budgets to go out and catch criminals.

Novels and stories about the police officer came slightly after the rise of the police force in nineteenth-century Europe. In France, such stories predated this slightly, because the police force was established as a separate entity from the army after the French Revolution. A transitional tale such as Victor Hugo's *Les Misérables* first began this pattern. It is, in a very clear sense, a police tale; but the protagonist is really a military figure who is given the function of working as a police officer. Unlike the private-detective tale, the public-detective or police tale has, until the last twenty or thirty years, received relatively little attention as a literary form. We have private-detective tales going back to Edgar Allan Poe's *Murders in the Rue Morgue,* in 1841, and the Sherlock Holmes tales, which began in 1891; and there are turn-of-the-century books about the history and interpretation of crime and detection. However, police tales—and many existed in the last century—were presented as true-crime reports and not as literature or fiction, in spite of the degree of latitude the authors often gave themselves.

One reason that critical interest in police tales has arisen more recently has been the large number of police-oriented television series. They became a clearly important cultural phenomenon. Initial critical attention to these police tales centered around whether or not they were accurate in their depiction of police work and whether they were too violent, and not around their interpretation as myth or fantasy. Because they do not detail actual police experience the failure to treat the police tale as a generic fantasy inhibited serious attention. We, however, will examine these television programs as fictional creations. As such we can expect them to tell us more about the fantasy life of the audience than the experience of police officers. We will begin by noting a difference between two types of police tale.

In one type of tale, we have a traditional policeman who shares many characteristics of the classical private detective, such as Sherlock Holmes or Agatha Christie's Hercule Poirot. These tales follow the police detective as he or she solves a crime or crimes. In literature, there are many examples: Georges Simenon's Inspector Maigret, Peter Lovesy's Sergeant Cribb, John Creasy's Gideon series, and Alan Hunter's Inspector Gently. There is even an Australian procedural detective, Napoleon Bonaparte, created by Arthur Upfield, and a pair of such detectives in Hong Kong, created by William Marshall in his Yellow Thread Street novels. Such tales were established on television by Jack Webb's "Dragnet" and include programs like "Starsky and Hutch,"

"Kojak," "Baretta," "Stone," "Paris," and "Eischied." What is stressed in these tales which differs from classical private-detective tales is the proletarian nature of the detective, who does not have great intellectual power like Sherlock Holmes or Hercule Poirot. What he does have is an understanding of the human condition and a feeling for other people. The very commonness of these detectives dictates how they proceed.

Another type of police tale involves uniformed police and is quite different in plot conventions and presentation from other crime tales. Those differences are tied to how closely the police officer is related to the institution of government. "Police Story," "Adam 12," "The Rookies," "T. J. Hooker," and "Chips" are all examples of the uniformed-police tale, which might be traced back to shows like "Highway Patrol" from the early 1950s.

Interestingly, "Hill Street Blues" has attempted to deal with both uniformed and plain-clothes officers. In doing so it has drawn its characters and conventions from both police tale formulas.

Characteristics of Police Protagonists

In plain clothes or uniform, the central character in a police tale has an inevitable commitment to averageness or the status quo. Related to this is the convention that the police detective is not highly intelligent. Intelligence is not a part of television's heroic definition of the police officer. As will be discussed later, "Columbo" is an interesting exception to the rule. He is both intelligent and grossly common. The virtue and possible defect of the police detective are his commitment to the rule of law and the protection of the populace, which can often become obsessive. If, for example, the police officer has a family, there is a danger to the familial situation itself in the police officer's commitment to the job.

In some ways the police tale has become an urban substitute for the Western. Interestingly, as in the Western, the hero on early cop shows was inevitably male. But in recent years shows like "Police Woman," "Cagney and Lacy," and "Hill Street Blues" have offered female protagonists within what was once an exclusively male community. Potentially interesting work remains to be done exploring the differences between television's male and female cops.

Another characteristic of both uniform and nonuniform tales is the importance of partnership. One does not work alone. One is part of a social group. Again, this is quite different from the private detective forms. Private detectives do not need partners. They traditionally work alone—or with somebody who is not an equal. In "The Rockford Files," the people supposedly helping the detective are usually more of an impediment than an aid. But the police officer is dependent on other people. There is a primary relationship with a partner or team. The work situation duplicates a familial situation. Relationships within the work situation become the primary social support for police officers; they live within their job. Many episodes of "Police Story" or "Hill Street Blues" involve a scene in which the neglected spouse and family say, "You spend more time with your partner than you do with me." Work becomes an alternate and important way of living. The partnership is established as one of dependent parts. The police tend to be successful only when they get along and work together. When one is removed, the others become vulnerable.

The Nature of the Criminal in Police Tales

The officer's relationship to the police force seems to depend on the nature of the criminal. Much of the criticism of the police tales on television stresses that, with the exception of some uniformed-police tales, the shows do not deal with the real nature of most crime. The criticism is, in one sense, quite true. The overwhelming number of criminal cases, in actuality, are domestic cases: people harming people they know. This and petty crime take up most police time. However, the police tale we see on television is not about real crime and never has been. In television, the overwhelming majority of crimes fall into two categories that are mythically important but exist only in very small numbers in actuality. The two kinds of criminals *predominantly* presented on television are individual lunatics and organized-crime figures. Some shows obviously tend toward other forms. "Hawaii Five-O" had a series of shows about criminal masterminds, but even they were treated as lunatics. Thus, the shows supposedly about crime are to a great extent not about the crime the real police normally encounter. They present, instead, a mythology about crimes that are symbolically important to the viewer.

Organized crime and individual madness are diametric opposites. Each represents something different, and the police officers must handle each of them in different ways. When the show defines the criminal as an insane individual, the police detective tends to grow more and more alienated from other officers. The central detective moves away from his or her partner and other members of the team and becomes obsessed with catching the madman. Since the detective team represents a unified whole, the existence of the lunatic, who is a fragmented, psychotic personality, mocks the existence of the team and social response to the threat he poses. The protagonist, in dealing with a madman, comes more and more to see the madman as a disease to be wiped out and often as a reflection of the officer's own dark side. The protagonist becomes impelled toward operating the way the madman operates. The officer moves outside of the law toward emotion and violence. On television, the story does not move to final confrontation as at the end of a film like *Dirty Harry*, where Harry throws his badge away. Ultimately in television—which is more socially reaffirming than film—the officer is pulled back and rejoins his supportive group before he commits an act that will separate him from society. But still, the lunatic is a kind of divisive force, threatening the cooperative effort.

When the criminal is a member of organized crime, on the other hand, the detective tends to work more closely with the members of his group. The criminal organization is presented as paralleling the police organization, so that there are two institutionalized forces opposing each other. What usually leads to the downfall of organized crime in a police tale is the criminal body's need for directions from above. If the police can get the key figure at the top, everything crumbles. This is not necessarily the way "The Syndicate" works in life; but, mythically, it works that way in the shows, because organized crime is presented as a patriarchy. Rarely is there a woman at the top.

Interaction of Police and Criminals

The police, in contrast, are very well trained and can function without a hierarchy. The criminals are totally dependent on their hierarchy, their own rules. The police can be hampered by the rules of law; but, unlike the criminals, they are not dependent on their hierarchy. There is no single person a criminal can "get" in the police force and stop an investigation.

When the police go after "Mr. Big," they are hampered because they have to work within the law. In the confrontation between a police officer and a member of organized crime, the criminal will frequently say, "You can't touch me; I know my rights. I'll plead the Fifth Amendment. I want a lawyer." The police are then totally frustrated, because this prevents them from protecting society. They may stretch the law, but they are ultimately fettered by it. In contrast, organized crime is limited by the fact that, once the key person is eliminated, supposedly the whole structure falls.

Both the organized-crime figures and the lunatics are presented as being intellectually superior to the police. What the police have going for them is a commitment to law and, even more important, a commitment to the populace, to protecting the people. They have the determination to persevere, to protect the people. They are not tireless, but they are replaceable. It is determination, not intellect, which allows them to overcome the criminals.

Conflict between Order and Individualism

The police in all media, unlike the classical private detectives such as Sherlock Holmes, also tend to renounce parental figures, a captain or commissioner. Ultimately, the protagonist doesn't need or want to accept the advice of this parental figure. The officer knows the right thing to do. The captain or commissioner can warn the officer, but this parental figure knows there are times when one doesn't obey superiors, when it is more important to act to protect the populace. This ambivalence between the idea of law and order and the police officer's need to move outside its limits to protect society relates to a basic motif of the Western. The poor police officer, who is not very intelligent in the first place, suddenly must decide whether to abandon the commitment to the law or stay within the law and maybe not protect the populace. The moment of anguish that exists over and over again in these police tales is that moment in which the protagonist has to make this decision. In a continuing series, the myth demands that whatever the officer decides will be made right. If the officer moves outside the law or ignores orders from the commander, the narrative will affirm that decision. On the other hand, if he decides to stay with the law, that decision is affirmed. No matter what is done it is the right thing.

Police as Lower-Middle-Class Heroes

Social class is very important in police tales, as it is in all kinds of crime tales. Classical detectives, from Sherlock Holmes to a contemporary TV example like "Hart to Hart," are of a higher social class. They mingle with, or are, aristocrats and rich people and are called in because they have special talents and special abilities. On the other

Betty Thomas as Sergeant Lucy Bates in ''Hill Street Blues.''

hand detectives like Mike Hammer or Thomas Magnum are very strongly middle-class and slightly outside of society. Former criminals like McCormick in "Hardcastle and McCormick," ex-cops like Harry Orwell, or old men like Barnaby Jones are marginal men with a commitment to a task which takes them outside of society. But television's cops invariably fall within a limited category of age and class. They are presented as lower-middle-class, and they are committed to protecting the values of that group. They want to protect life and property, but property is particularly important. The villains aspire to money and freedom, which the policemen can never have. The police accept their limitations. They are committed to working within the structure. They give up both their time and their freedom.

"Columbo" was very much like a classical detective tale, in that the protagonist was matched with someone worthy of him, which is quite different from typical police tales. The criminals think Columbo is bumbling, but we know that he's not. In fact, in some Columbo episodes his superior I.Q. is mentioned. He is intellectually superior; yet, at the same time, he is committed to protecting the lower middle class: his car, the way he talks about his wife and his mother-in-law, the way he dresses and talks—all represent commitments to that image of middle-classness. Because he is so committed to the social norm, the upper-class criminal tends to underrate him initially and then upgrade him only when it is too late.

Columbo had a foot in both the classical private-detective tradition and the cop formula. Unlike the average cop-show cop, he did things that most of us could not do. Usually, we could do whatever these people do if we were willing to risk our lives. In fact, we might be able to do it better than they do it. They might be physically stronger than we are, but certainly they are not smarter, whereas Columbo was obviously smarter than we are. Typical television cops almost never have information the audience does not have. The shows, in fact, usually start by giving the viewer information unknown to the cop, by showing us who the criminal is, and perhaps how the crime was committed. In contrast, television mysteries which follow the conventions of the classical private detective tale, such as "Nero Wolfe," "Ellery Queen," and "Hart to Hart," let neither the audience nor the detective know who the criminal is.

In police tales, criminals are seeking something from the society that the policeman and his contemporaries do not have. Criminals, at least in organized crime, have and desire vast amounts of money. The policeman, and by mythic extension, the audience, could be expected not to like people who have freedom or money that they are denied by the restrictions of law, morality, and convention. Corruption in cop tales is very specific. Somebody is the bad guy, and we know who it is; he gets caught, and that is the end of the evil. In other kinds of tales, evil can be very nebulous. Unlike the hard-boiled story and most certainly unlike real life, on the typical cop show, guilt is clear and specific.

Narrative Pattern

The narrative pattern which activates the formula and identifies guilt and innocence is quite clear, though there are some variations. Usually, the first thing we see is the crime being committed. We have information immediately that the police don't have, and so our experience differs from theirs.

The next important narrative motif is that the cop is assigned to the case by chance. The cop has no personal ties to the case. Joe Friday will say, "We were working the night watch out of Rialto, when. . . ." Or Ponch and John happen to be standing nearby when the madman captures the stewardess.

Then the destruction widens. The madman kills another businessman wearing a neat trenchcoat, or the organized criminal beats up one more Italian restaurant owner. Whatever, the crimes become even more personal for the cop. As the crimes expand, they start happening to people who represent something particular and personal to the police officer.

If the tale is long enough, the officer starts neglecting personal life (to the extent that such exists), and the quest for the criminal becomes more and more obsessive. The cop behaves less and less rationally.

The next step, which does not necessarily come at this point, is that the detective meets the criminal. Sometimes they meet by chance, and the detective doesn't know that this is the criminal or murderer. Sometimes the cop does know but does not have the evidence to hold the culprit. But there is a confrontation; and then the criminal is lost, after following an initial chase. This is often followed by a warning. Somebody (spouse, partner, superior) says to the police officer, "Don't lose your perspective. You are a police officer; you are dedicated to certain principles." The warning is, of course, ignored.

The next step involves following the trail. The officer has to get through levels of society in an attempt to get to the criminal, talking to the rich or the poor, bartenders, taxi drivers, rooming house owners, bums, and company presidents. This leads ultimately to a direct, open, physical confrontation with the criminal. Usually, this is the second confrontation, particularly in a one-hour television show. Very frequently, this takes place in an urban arena, a place where the two can challenge each other in mock gladiatorial combat.

The last narrative step in the formula is that the police destroy or capture the villain. The overwhelming tendency in television is not to destroy, but to capture, to contain and control the symbol of evil.

In the course of these tales, the police tend to meet various nearly allegorical character types. Five kinds of characters will be suggested here, not necessarily the kinds of characters a cop really encounters but characters of the police mythology.

Typical Characters

One frequent character is the *informer*, the contact, the connection with the underworld. Frequently, the informer turns out to be an unreliable mediator between the criminals and the cops. Informers are not connected to the underworld. They are comic-tragic figures on the fringes of two worlds, neither of which accepts them fully. The police officer, when dealing with the informer, must rely on skill and experience to determine the degree to which the informer can be trusted.

The cop invariably encounters *criminals*. Strangely enough, media cops are comfortable with criminals and in the criminal environment. This is the cop's manageable environment, something despised but understood. Often, this attachment to the criminals and their world will be emphasized in a retirement show about a uniformed cop. What will the cop do in retirement, removed from criminals who have determined the meaning of his life? Retiring cuts the officer off from two important relationships: other police officers and criminals. Ultimately, what these retirees say is, "I like being with you guys so much; you're my family, and I really need criminals so much that if I am forced to retire, I will kill myself." To lose the image of one's dark side, to sever the connection to someone outside oneself who can take on all one's projections of evil, is devastating to the cop.

The cop regularly encounters *middle-class people*, frequently storekeepers or small-business owners. These are the very people the cop is most committed to protecting, for they share conformist images.

The cop's respect for them is clear, though they are usually the least defined characters in the tale. The middle-class representatives remain a kind of nebulous projection of the American urban scene that is supposed to be protected.

Contrasted with the middle class are the members of the *upper class*. For the police, this is the group of people to whom one must be most deferential and with which cops are least able to deal. They are uncomfortable and awkward with rich people, who represent an environment based on wealth and power within which the police officer, who thrives on power, is weak or helpless.

An important group that the police officer encounters and deals with in these tales is the *officer's own family*. A frequent irony in police tales is that the officer is unable to handle the family the way he or she can handle the criminal world. On "Hill Street Blues," in recent seasons partners Hill and Renko have had difficult relations with their fathers, Furillo can't handle his ex-wife and Belker has ongoing problems with his mother. On the job they are professionals, but at home they fall apart. Their erratic private lives contrast with their control of their professional lives. Their work is ordered by rules and obligations, but their family lives require interpersonal relationships, which they invariably can't handle. In police tales, home is a place where you go when you must.

Setting

Cop tales are almost exclusively urban. This does not mean there are no stories about rural police officers and contemporary sheriffs; but, on television and in movies, the noncomic cop is presented as a city figure. There have not been many tales about the cops in small towns except comic ones like "Andy Griffith," "Carter Country," "Enos," and "Lobo." In dialogue and presentation, the city is presented as a potential jungle, a perverted primitive environment. The word *jungle* occurs repeatedly. The cop is presented as a keeper of the law, a total conformist. Conformity is needed to contain the animalism in the city. That metaphor carries through again and again, most strikingly, perhaps, in a film like *Escape from New York* in which Manhattan itself becomes a vast urban jungle. This poor, beleaguered middle-class figure has no great intellectual capacity, but does possess the determination to save the city from the animals.

Tools of the Trade

The police officer has three primary tools that recur in the cop shows: the gun, particular clothes, and the automobile.

The police officer typically has a greater skill with the gun than do the criminals. Over the course of the years, the handling of the gun has changed in police tales. Before Vietnam, the policeman stood, almost dispassionately, with his side to the target and the pistol at arm's length while he sighted down the barrel. Now, the officer holds the gun with two hands and crouches facing the target head-on. This has been universally accepted on television as the professional stance, the posture of training rather than that of the Western gunfight.

Normally, the gun is a symbol of order in the hands of a police officer. He or she has to be very careful not to abuse the gun. At the same time, the gun represents the potential paranoia of the police officer, the ordinary person who has to make decisions all the time, to "fire the gun/don't fire the gun." In episode after episode, an officer fires, shoots someone, and has to go before a board of inquiry to justify why he or she did it. The cop's partner or partners must go out and find a bullet in an alley or someone who fired from a window to free the tainted officer from public guilt.

With a few exceptions, the "uniforms" of the detectives are nondescript. Their clothes are as inconspicuous as possible; not necessarily because they are hiding, but because those are the clothes that they choose to wear. They dress as they are, lower-middle class, white-collar workers. One can't say, "Ah, that is a suit that McGarrett would wear," because, if you said that, you'd just be picking a suit off the rack. There's no special identification to that kind of suit. There are a few variations. Baretta definitely dressed, lived, and acted lower-class rather than lower-middle-class. The whole "Baretta" set duplicated the idea that he was a lower-class character, whereas the majority of police in the media are lower-middle-class characters.

The antagonists, the bad guys, dress differently. Animalistic madmen, pimps, and petty criminals, because they are free of society's constraints, dress bizarrely. They have freedom to be conspicuous. Successful organized-crime figures, however, usually dress the same as the cops, only better. They too wear clothing that is not conspicuous, but it is of a better quality: tailor-made suits rather than the ones the cops buy off the racks. In the Western, the protagonist, both by dress and physical appearance, often stood out from the crowd. There is a particular, rugged Western look that the audience expects; but a cop can look like anybody. Police officers are presented as average people who blend into the crowd.

The automobile can be paralleled with the horse in a Western. The importance of the automobile in police tales could be overestimated, but it is presented as the deadliest urban artifact in the police officer's domain. As the cowboy knows how to handle a horse, the cop can handle an automobile. But unlike the cowboy with his horse, the police officer does not respect the automobile. There is no love for it. In "Starsky and Hutch," there was a running joke that Hutch cared about his automobile. But the traditional position is that the police car is a hunk of interchangeable machinery the officer knows how to operate, a tool to be used. In the car chase, the cop gets a chance to display greater mastery of the automobile, and hence the urban environment, than the criminal has. While they obviously do not occur in every episode, the car chases recur as a mythic expression of this mastery of the environment. The same thing can be seen in the cowboy's mastery of his horse. If the cowboy prevails in his chase, it is because he rides better than the bad guy, knows the terrain, and can shoot better. He has greater control over the iconic tools within his kind of tale. The police officer is supposed to have better control over automobiles and guns than the villain has. Frequently, there are two chases: an initial chase in which the officer suffers a defeat; and then the longer chase, which parallels the first, in which the cop is successful.

Other tools, like the two-way radio or the computer, sometimes appear to evidence the police's control over technology. On "Hawaii Five-O" the police constantly used computers, radios, cameras, all sorts of gadgets. When they were on the radio, they had access to a whole network of help, to which the bad guys did not have access. In "Adam-12," it was quite clear that the cops were not particularly intelligent. What protected them was that they worked within a group, knew the procedures, and acted accordingly.

The Police Story as Tragedy

The presentation of crime and the police on television is one in which the police officer faces an overwhelming situation. It takes everything the officer has to keep up with it. Ultimately, these tales are a kind of lower-middle-class tragedy. The police must suffer for society, risk their own sanity and their lives and loved ones.

One important recurring aspect of police tales, even on television, is their nonconclusive nature—as opposed to "Remington Steele," "Hardcastle and McCormick," or any of the private-eye tales. These police tales imply that tracking down criminals never ends. Very frequently, we are informed that there are a number of crimes going on at the same time. McGarrett calls in one of his helpers, who says, "I'm working on the murder down at the docks." Kojak will say, "Get off of that hijacking, because you've got to help me." In "Adam-12" or "Hill Street Blues" there are literally a number of crimes being attended to. Every "Police Story" ended with the implication that a new crime had begun. We heard a voice on the radio announcing a new crime in progress, a situation quite different from the classical tale in which, at the close of the story, Sherlock Holmes locates the specific villain. Ultimately, a private detective such as Holmes will get everybody together, figure out who the criminal is, and then allow the police to grab the person and lock him up. Social order is restored. In our urban police mythology, however, as in our lives, criminal activity never stops.

—7—

A Structural Analysis of the Police Story

by Dennis Giles

Art may imitate life but does not reproduce it. A story is always more organized than life; it presents a heightened reality. According to Alfred Hitchcock, a satisfying story is a "slice of cake" rather than a slice of life. No fiction script can stand up to the test of plausibility or credibility. Popular television genres, like popular films and novels, rarely detail the "average everydayness" of experience, to use a phrase from the German philosopher Martin Heidegger, but instead the experience that matters—events that change the direction of human life. "What is drama, after all," Hitchcock said repeatedly, "but life with the dull bits cut out."

The Study of Narrative Structure

Aristotle defines plot as "simply this, the combination of the incidents, or things done in the story." But events do not follow one another in random succession in the narrative chain. They are organized according to a certain logic—not the logic of "real life," but storytelling logic.

The study of narrative structure tries to describe those rules of combination which organize events into a coherent story. This approach considers plot as a passage—not only a journey from place to place, but a passage between states of mind, states of being. It treats the story as a movement from an original imbalance (of justice, for example) to the resolution of that imbalance which provides the sense of a satisfactory ending. If a fiction is both a model of reality and a remodeling of previous fiction within the same genre, the student of narrative constructs a model of the story itself—a model of the model—to discover the laws which move the story from its opening promise of an event that matters through the crisis which fulfills the promise. In other words, the narrative analyst studies the story as a structure in process of transformation. Yet the analysis of the actions and events which form a plot is often so abstract that it bears little relation to the actual experience of watching and hearing—understanding and feeling—a story.

Television and Folk Art

In his pioneering study of 100 Russian *marchen* (fairy tales), *The Morphology of the Folktale,* Vladimir Propp was able to transform each plot into a sequence of algebraic notations: *F* (the hero gains use of a magical agent), *H* (combat with the villain), *Pr* (the hero is pursued), *Ex* (the false hero is exposed), *U* (the villain is punished), etc. Propp discovered thirty-one "functions," or acts, possible in any one story, some of which could be omitted, repeated, or rearranged to generate new tales. Each actual folktale is understood as a variation upon a single model. Propp was interested in a particular instance of storytelling only for what it told him about the narrative rules of the whole genre of folktales. Because genre analysis necessarily generalizes, individual differences between stories are often lost in the attempt to discern a common pattern of events. The analyst sees the forest clearly but neglects the concrete presence of the trees.

Despite its abstractions, the *Morphology* has heavily influenced the study of classical "heroic" texts and popular narratives. Propp's discovery that the typical plot is *curative,* that it enacts the hero's attempt to remedy a fundamental deficiency or "lack" in his or her world, is a particularly useful way of thinking about the police story. While the heroes and villains of folktales move in an idealized space, cut off from the world, the police genre attempts to root its fiction in the mean streets of everyday life. Yet, despite its emphasis upon realism, the police story replays the central acts of the folktale. Both are clearly action genres, emphasizing chases, combats, and the play of weapons. Both the traditional folktale and the police story begin their plots with the violation of law and/or the hero's transgression of a prohibition.

In each genre, the audience is expected to admire and identify with a protagonist who displays special powers and abilities, and yet is simultaneously an everyman.

Although television programs are highly calculated commercial products, they share many of the characteristics of anonymous "folk art." In both television and the folktale, the creativity or inventiveness that is the mark of value in the fine arts is subordinated to the replay of conventions. Of course, to some extent, all artistic expression restates a previous communication and plays variations on an earlier text. No art work can possibly "make sense" to an audience unless it is based upon certain conventions shared by both the artist and the culture. Yet, in most forms of artistic communication, the requirement to speak in the inherited, conventional language is always in tension with the producer's desire to invent a new form of expression. An episode of "Police Story" and the Greek tragedy are each the product of a compromise between convention and invention.

Whether an artistic production is classified as popular or "fine" art depends, to a large extent, upon its degree of fidelity to a previous model. The artist who stresses creation over repetition gains cultural prestige at the same time that the audience is limited to an educated elite. But, like the artist of the medieval and classical ages, the producer of television dramas gains a large audience by playing variations on a repertory of well-known conventions. The pleasure of genre productions comes both from our recognition of familiar territory and our trust that the rules of the game are flexible enough to admit new forms of play.

Television is conservative in its storytelling, spinning off new series from proven successes, updating traditional plots that preexist the medium by centuries. But TV genres are rarely brittle structures shattered by the pressure of new material, new styles of expression. Viable genres like the police story function as open, dynamic systems, always in process of renewal, while yet remaining themselves. The authoritarian, fiercely middle-class Ironside yields to the scruffy proletarian figure of Baretta as the genre begins to tolerate—even champion—deviant life-styles. The stern, no-nonsense face of Jack Webb as Joe Friday ("Just the facts, ma'am") is replaced by the seductive, let's-fool-around grin of Erik Estrada on "Chips" as strictly defined case assignments yield to the free-wheeling patrols of the motorcycle cop. While the private lives of the cops in "Dragnet" and "The F.B.I." are clearly distinct from their professional functions, "Police Story," "Cagney and Lacy," and "Hill Street Blues" cops bring their jobs home, as the walls between public and private worlds become increasingly porous.

Characteristics of the Police-Story Plot

The police story is a plot of restoration. The world is thrown into a state of imbalance by criminal action. While patrolling his beat, the cop discovers the violation of law or is dispatched from the station to the scene of the crime. (Propp's functions *A, B, C,* $\uparrow$: the villain causes a lack, the lack is "made known," the hero begins counter-action or is dispatched to the scene, the hero departs on his journey.) After various preliminary combats (Propp's "test scenes") and the interrogation of witnesses, suspects, informers (the characters Propp describes as "helpers"), the criminal is met and vanquished in the field of battle, though the hero is often wounded in the process (functions *H,J,I,K:* combat with the villain, the hero "branded" in the fight, the villain defeated, the lack is "liquidated"). The plot has come full circle—the reign of justice has been restored. The cop returns home to the station or the familiar grounds of his beat, where he is rewarded—if only by a pat on the back—for a job well done (functions $\downarrow$,*Q,W:* the hero returns, is recognized, and "ascends the throne").

The policeman combines the roles of the *seeking* hero and the *victim* hero. As an investigator, he is involved in a search for knowledge or an object of value; e.g., a kidnap victim. Yet, he is also the victim of assaults on his person. The policeman seeks retribution, attempting to pay back the criminal in his own violent coin. The plot structure detailed above is played as a specifically *police* story by utilizing the plot devices of a *crime,* an *investigation, preliminary combats,* and a single, *final combat.*

The Crime

The criminal attacks a private citizen, a policeman, or both. When the cop is dispatched to a crime in progress, the criminal redirects his attack from the original victim to the representative of the law. As a result, the cop becomes a second victim, so that the gravity of the original crime is doubled. This direct attack on the law sharpens the conflict, transforming a story of routine, impersonal justice into a drama of private (yet legal) revenge. In theory, the police function is simply surveillance, pursuit, and capture; punishment is left to the courts and the prisons. However, the police genre often assumes that the courts pervert the story of justice by refusing really to punish the criminal. As a cop bitterly complains in an episode of "Police Story": "That's what gets me. You catch him in the act and he's out in twenty-four hours. Out until the trial. If there *is* a trial! And they buy themselves super lawyers. . . ."

In innumerable stories, the police are "forced" to usurp the function of judge and jury. The genre typically narrates an opposed and equal reply to criminal violence. Doubts as to whether the police should themselves punish the criminal or leave him to the mercy of the courts are effectively resolved when the criminal leaves the cop "no choice" but to shoot back in self-defense. As an experienced policeman explains to his chief in "Police Story," "You know and I know that the only way to stop these people is to put them down." Punishment is more clearly possible than rehabilitation and a rookie cop is likely to be told, "If you have some kind of desire to save souls, get yourself transferred to juvenile."

In some forms of the genre ("Baretta"), the cop consciously considers himself to be the victim's personal delegate in a quest for revenge rather than the cool enforcer of an essentially impersonal law; because the individual victim is neither licensed nor qualified to avenge the injury, the policeman performs a public act of retribution. In other stories, the original victim rapidly disappears from a field of combat dominated entirely by the police and the criminal teams. In such cases, the cop does not represent the citizens so much as the interests of his own professional organization. Rather than impartially applying society's law, he seeks vengeance for the death of a brother officer or seeks a reply to assaults on the prestige of the special family he represents.

The Investigation and Preliminary Combats (Tests)

In the police story, these two action sequences are often intertwined. They both complicate the plot and build the sense of frustration to be released in the terminal catharsis of the gunfight. The hero advances toward his goal; but, at the same time, his action is blocked by the storyteller. The plot rarely progresses in a straight line but circles backward at the very moment when the solution seems clearly in view. In the first major sequence of the "Police Story" episode just cited, a carefully laid ambush by "special unit" forces is ruined by a rookie's mistake, allowing a vicious character named Slowboy to take a woman hostage during a holdup attempt. Although Slowboy surrenders when the senior cop threatens to shoot through his human shield, the criminal is later freed on bail. In the remainder of the plot, the unit prepares an elaborate trap by which they can finally "waste" Slowboy, thus correcting the error of the legal system, while the rookie learns to master the mysteries of "special tactics." The introductory confrontation has proven to be only a test combat in which we learn the nature of the antagonist and discover precisely what abilities the hero must possess in order to qualify properly for the heroic role.

The decision to emphasize test combats or an investigative journey depends primarily on whether the identity of the criminal is known to police. Whereas "Dragnet" and "Ironside" episodes often detailed the step-by-step solution of a mystery, by the 1970s the mainstream of the genre had become the story of pursuit (particularly in Quinn Martin's "The F.B.I.," 1965-74). The popular *undercover* variation of the *pursuit story* reverses the classic situation of the public cop versus an unknown antagonist. The undercover cop ("Police Woman") is the deceiver—the charming trickster—operating secretly in the heart of the criminal world. The problem is no longer one of recognizing the criminal, but of preventing one's own recognition until the moment of truth—the scene of open combat. Yet, in both the classic and undercover variations of the genre, the spectator fully shares the cop's knowledge (or lack of it); we may be partners in deception *with* the cop, but we are never deceived by him.

In the process of investigation, the protagonist further proves his heroic qualifications by demonstrating courage, persistence, "street smarts" (intuition)—all those qualities that separate him from "the others." (Simply dominating the TV image is not sufficient to qualify a man for heroism: his image must be *filled in* with individual and generic traits; i.e., he must be stamped with character.) Whether the police story stresses investigation or combat, it usually combines the two activities in a single narrative. Whatever the mix, the investigative journey per se is studded with scenes of *interrogation*. These can be understood as displacements (and restatements) of the physical tests that dominate the pursuit variation of the genre.

Interrogation is a verbal form of combat that directly prepares the final resolution. In order to force valuable information from a reluctant suspect or "snitch," the police threaten, promise, and cajole. The interrogation is a version of the scene in so many myths where the journeying hero is blocked by a creature from another world who challenges him to a contest. This often fabulous creature offers crucial advice, a magical weapon, or a password only if the hero can successfully answer a riddle, strike an appropriate bargain, win a wrestling match, etc. Such characters, called *helpers* by Propp, are neither clearly on the side of the hero nor allies of the villainous forces; like "Rooster," the flamboyant black pimp/informer in "Baretta," they appear as independent operators trying to maintain relations with both worlds.

Both Oedipus's Sphinx and the policeman's snitch are devious by nature. Their answers must be carefully interpreted as ambiguous signs that point toward truth; the informer/oracle rarely tells (or knows) the *full* truth. The cop depends upon this network of pseudo-information because he can only *visit* the criminal underworld, never fully *live* in it. (Even as an undercover agent in the criminal homeland, the policeman is only a tourist.) The care and feeding of snitches, squealers, and other contacts is an ubiquitous subplot of the police genre.

The Final Combat (Test)

Fear is a dominant emotion of melodrama. In the police story, the moment of greatest fear (thus the greatest sense of drama) occurs in those crucial seconds in which the warrior is cut off from his brothers, facing his murderous antagonist one on one. Previous scenes of camaraderie, horseplay with fellow officers, and the exchange of confidences between partners in the squad car all serve to heighten, by contrast, the fear of being alone. The cop is an organization man by training and habit, emotionally dependent on the communication from other policemen and the dispatcher at "home base." The coded squawk of the radio accompanies him everywhere, assuring him that the rest of the team is "in touch." Normally, the cop rests secure in the knowledge that the call "officer needs assistance" will, within minutes, bring a swarm of guns and uniforms to the point of crisis. But in those few terrible minutes, the cop must live or die as an individual, shut off from the support of his comrades-in-arms. The scene of sudden and perilous isolation is stressed in the police story, not only because it contrasts so dramatically with the "brotherhood" that defines the cop's normal experience, but because at this moment, the genre speaks in a much older tradition of storytelling. From the wars of the Old Testament or the *Iliad* to the aerial dogfight films like *Hell's Angels* and *Star Wars,* the final test that makes or breaks a warrior-hero is the challenge of single combat. Joseph Wambaugh's titles *The New Centurions* and "The Blue Knight" (a made-for-TV movie and a TV series) explicitly recognize that a tradition even more ancient than feudal sagas of valor still informs the combat genres as a whole, and the police story in particular. Although the policeman acts as a member of a team through most of the plot, there is no point in qualifying and individualizing this hero unless he moves into the arena of death *on his own.* According to the tradition, at the critical moment of his story, the blue knight must fight alone, or the story is simply not worth telling.

Chips: The Pure Pursuit

The "Red Rider" episode (1980) of "Chips" begins with a pretitle sequence in which a masked bandit rides his motorcycle on the sidewalk of the prestigious Rodeo Drive shopping area in Beverly Hills, smashes a jewelry store window, snatches an expensive necklace in front of astonished onlookers, and then guns his cycle to make a fast escape. Motorcycle cop Ponch pursues, but the thief's cycle is far more powerful. Ponch crashes his cycle, having failed the first test combat.

The title sequence alternates wide shots of the two heroes with close detail shots of guns, badges, motorcycle wheels, and an extreme close-up of a booted foot. All shots are taken from a moving camera as the motorcycle cops speed together down a four-lane highway, informing the viewer that this will be a *mobile* story.

The next two sequences repeat and vary the original action in order to demonstrate a fundamental deficiency: the heroes do not possess the right tools to bring the criminal to justice. While Ponch recovers from his wounds in a hospital bed, his partner John twice pursues the criminal only to be frustrated by the limits of his own motorcycle. The two cops briefly investigate by reminiscing about a previous episode in the series in which they encountered a similar "supercycle." They conclude that the criminal is probably "The Fabulous Phantom"—star of a motorcycle thrills show—because only this old antagonist could possibly possess the equipment and skill to escape three desperate pursuits by professionals. Verbal contests with The Phantom at the site of the thrill show fail to gain information or victory. The Phantom denies guilt; the police hunch is not yet evidence.

Late in the third sequence, curative action begins. In order to put the law on equal terms with the criminal, John demands and receives the police supercycle. Now that the imbalance of power has been remedied, the plot will be won or lost by skill alone. Mounted on his fabulous machine, John outperforms his opponent in the final pursuit. When the mask is stripped from the criminal, we discover that he is not The Phantom but a jealous assistant on the support team of the thrills show. Consumed with envy, the Red Rider wished to prove "in real life" that he could equal The Phantom's exploits on the track.

In this youth-oriented variation of the pursuit subgenre, the police are rarely forced to use their guns. The gun is replaced by the motorcycle as the means by which the criminal is captured. In fact, the cycle functions as a weapon, and the title sequence includes more close-ups of the cycle than of the gun. Both the capture and the crime are bloodless and relatively nonviolent. The victim is a jewelry store, not an individual; it sells luxuries to a social elite and can presumably afford the loss. The only injuries sustained by anyone are suffered during the pursuit: Ponch's accident is a result of his own actions, completely unintended by the criminal, while the major wound is to police pride. Both Ponch and John are shamed by the loss of the test combats; the supercycle is clearly the instrument by which the cops can resurrect their lost prestige. "Red Rider" is not so much a story of crime and justice as a contest of machines.

"Chips" can be seen as the police version of the so-called professional variation of the Western, in which the hero is no longer morally superior to his antagonist but is merely the representative of an opposing team. In this battle of speed, skill, and machinery, the police are the superior players; the moral struggle between good and evil has been transformed into a sports contest.

The Cop, the Organization

> But just as pure gold hath only a decorative purpose and for sterner uses must be alloyed with baser metals, so must the pure heart be made more sturdy by means of certain truths, which in themselves may be ignoble. To know evil sufficiently to fight against it, but not so well as to be infected by it, is the duty of the knight [Thomas Berger, *Arthur Rex: A Legendary Novel]*.

While the police hero displays special powers and abilities which differentiate him from "civilians"—ordinary citizens—he is simulta-

Efrem Zimbalist, Jr., in "The F.B.I."

Raymond Burr in "Ironside."

Efrem Zimbalist, Jr., and William Reynolds in "The F.B.I."

neously an *Everyman*. In contrast to superhuman crime fighters like Superman, the Hulk, and the Bionic Woman, the policeman is not exceptional by nature. He displays no magical powers, no charms; there is nothing uncanny about him. To be sure, he is set apart by his knowledge of death, by his use of death-dealing weapons. But the policeman's death, when it comes, is a mean, brutal death; when a cop is gunned down, the police story prefers to communicate pain—sheer human suffering. It is neither the policeman's birth, his wealth, nor his breeding that establishes his difference from ordinary men, but his professional function, symbolized by the gun and the badge. Representing the threat of lethal force and the ability to use it, these are precisely the emblems emphasized in the title sequence ("Chips," "Ironside," "Police Story," "Police Woman"). The cop is not born with power but has learned how to exercise it. Apprenticeship stories—training the rookie—regularly parallel the primary story of investigation/pursuit. Ironside, in particular, plays the firm parent who guides and corrects his mixed brood of youthful cops.

Unlike the intellectually superior "whodunit" detectives (Ellery Queen, Quincy and Ironside in some episodes), high-living, wisecracking private eyes ("Vegas"), or the international sophisticates played by Robert Wagner ("Switch," "Hart to Hart"), the typical cop is an unpolished man of the streets, with proletarian tastes. The semiliterate speech of Baretta proves that he can provide justice *for* the people because he is himself *of* the people:

> We're all scared, kid. I'm scared every day of my life. Not because I'm a cop, but because I'm a person. I guess we're all left holdin' da bag in dis world, kid. Dat's what they call livin'. But it beats dyin'.

Police stories work from egalitarian assumptions: the law applies equally to everyone; nobody is permitted to be an "exception" outside the reach of police authority. Although Columbo operates on the fringe of the genre (he works essentially alone, assembling clues on the model of the classical English detective), Columbo's achievement is typical of the policeman's work, because it cuts a rich, powerful criminal "down to size," demonstrating that not even the social elite are insulated from justice. "Baretta," "The F.B.I.," and "Police Woman" often perform a kind of democratic leveling by penetrating the defenses of the Mafia Don—the modern equivalent of an absolute monarch—who arrogantly believes himself to be invulnerable, above and beyond the law.

"The F.B.I." and "Police Story" represent the two extremes of the genre in their attitudes toward the police organization. In "The F.B.I.," the identity of the federal officer is entirely synonymous with his professional role. From the evidence of the series, this policeman has no private life; the organization makes the man. Strictly speaking, the federal cop is only an agent of the Bureau. As a limb of the body carries out instructions from the head, the field agent faithfully executes directives from Washington. Within this closed system, there is little free play for personal idiosyncrasies or private problems. Because the members of the organization are so disciplined, so firmly controlled, the very name *F.B.I.* pronounces the doom of the criminal. Like a force of destiny, like the impersonal Fate of Greek tragedy, the organization inexorably limits the freedom of criminal action until the trap is finally closed. "The F.B.I." represents the force of law raised to an infinite power, unrestricted by geographical boundaries or the flaws of personality. Within this context of organizational power, the series is hard-pressed to give Inspector Erskine (Efrem Zimbalist, Jr.) opportunities to individuate himself—to qualify as the hero. Erskine's role is purely representative; he is the visible face of the organization.

Although the field agents, headed by Erskine, are ostensibly the heroes of the "F.B.I." series, the character who occupies the screen for most of the drama is the criminal, not the cop. In fact, "The F.B.I." is more an *outlaw* story than a *police* story; it concentrates on the pathetic attempt of a small-time hoodlum to escape the jaws of justice. The natural opponent of the federal police organization is the only other organization that can match its power—the shadowy supergovernment called "The Mob," "The Syndicate," "The Mafia." When a massively efficient organization moves against a lone individual, the contest is simply unfair. Such a story violates the tradition that protagonist and antagonist must display approximately equal strength in order that the spectator can live in suspense for the duration of the story, pretending that the issue is in doubt. Yet, the Syndicate can never be annihilated by the F.B.I., or the organization loses its principal enemy, thus its very reason for existence. For every mafioso who is jailed, another takes his place. The Mob is as permanent as the F.B.I., although its faces may change. The organization remains the prime antagonist.

Since the Syndicate bosses can be linked only indirectly with any specific crime, Inspector Erskine and company focus upon the weakest links of the criminal family. The F.B.I. typically pursues low-level employees who will "finger" their immediate superiors in return for reduced sentences. Although the primary conflict is between two professional organizations, the "F.B.I." drama is triangulated (and personalized) by emphasizing the story of a criminal victim caught between the two centers of power. In other words, the strategy of "The F.B.I." is to divide the criminal role into two sets of characters, displacing the viewer's attention from the well-insulated, impersonal Syndicate to a relatively vulnerable, thus sympathetic, individual.

In "The Quarry" episode of "The F.B.I.," Michael Riley, a "runner for the Cosa Nostra," draws attention to himself by violently evading a federal roadblock. Fearful that he will inform on his bosses, the Mob arranges an assassination squad. From this point (the pretitle sequence) onward, the F.B.I. and the Cosa Nostra run a race respectively to save or to kill the unlucky fugitive, while the intended victim successfully evades both parties until the closing moments of the story. During the chase, Riley's trusting girlfriend is badly wounded by a Mafia bullet, while the pathos is further heightened by the victim's dream of a miraculous escape to "an island in Mexico" where the two lovers can live out their lives undisturbed by federal or mob law. The quarry is the classic man in the middle, pursued by both teams, desiring only to leave the game permanently. This outlaw is not a predator by nature or a professional criminal; he is the very antithesis of an organization man. As Riley's brother explains to Inspector Erskine, "He can't help you. He's a loner; thinks he doesn't need *anybody* else . . . except his girl."

The F.B.I. quarry is a variant of the romantic outlaw exemplified by (1) the rebels—Robin Hood, Zorro, Zapata, (2) the righteous bandits—Jesse James, Billy the Kid, (3) the victim-heroes of the *film noir,* and (4) the doomed lovers of the outlaw-couple genre (Bonnie and Clyde). These criminals have been placed on the wrong side of the law by a naive drive to find a private place in the sun; they are displaced persons, drifters, eternally homeless. Constitutionally unsuited for life in a "civilized" world of institutions, they are doomed to extinction by the organizations that enforce the law—mob law *or* federal law. According to the assumptions of "The F.B.I.," the desire to live one's own law is a universally seductive fantasy, but the life of the loner is impossible/illegal. Like it or not, we must adapt ourselves to the law of the organization, or the organization will destroy us.

In contrast to "The F.B.I.," where no quarrels of policy or procedure are allowed to interrupt the efficient application of justice, the organization is itself the battleground in "Police Story" and the later "Hill Street Blues." Like the social melodrama exhaustively analyzed by John Cawelti in *Adventure, Mystery and Romance,* "Police Story" offers the "inside story" of a powerful institution, exposing sometimes "the dirt" but always the personal drama hidden behind the public image. The series fragments the organization into competing power centers in which Vice wars with Homicide for jurisdiction over the murder of a prostitute or pimp. The organization is no longer the monolithic power structure of the F.B.I., but an arena where individuals jockey for prestige and choice assignments, unable to separate their off-duty roles from their professional duties. The "Police Story" concept, pioneered by Joseph Wambaugh, is to mix public and private spheres of life in volatile combination. The *outside* story of investigation on the streets is often only a catalyst to the *inside* story of a primary change in a cop's relations with his fellow officers, his wife, or his conscience.

Violence

The suspense of fiction is based on the delay of actions which the viewer knows are essential to the genre. The viewer's sense of satisfaction is dependent on his or her knowledge of where this story is going. The viewer does not know (or want to know) exactly how the promised scene will be played out but expects a resolution that makes sense within the rules of the genre. The implicit contract in force between the viewer and the television program demands that the viewer will be mildly surprised within the conventions, that this story will both replay and vary previous stories within the same genre. The viewing contract assumes that this particular episode of "Baretta" will be simultaneously new and familiar, that it will renew the genre without violating the viewer's fundamental expectations.

Although the police story, like every genre, is founded on a complex system of promises, the promise of violence is central to its specific climate of expectation. The cop wears a gun. He carries a nightstick. He moves in an atmosphere of violence—threats of violence, violence forecast and delivered. A fundamental definition of the policeman's role on television is his ability to respond to attacks on his person with an opposed and equal force. Violence is promised—connoted—by the very image of the cop. Yet, violence is "natural" to the genre, not only because the protagonist is an enforcer by profession, but also because his potentially lethal force is activated by the dramatic form in which he works. The cop may be a reluctant killer, essentially reactive in his violence; but his hand is forced by the requirements of melodrama.

In melodrama, as Robert Heilman writes, "one attacks or is attacked; it is always a kind of war." Melodramatic acts, by definition, are pushed to extremes. The conflict is unambiguous, simplified, purified, and typically drives breathlessly to a "just" ending. In tragedy, the protagonist can win while losing, or lose in the winning; but in the polarized world of melodrama, one plays to win everything—or loses one's life in the attempt. Melodrama is a zero-sum game that can only result in defeat or victory. If the police story is the drama of public justice (compared to the private justice of revenge dramas), its plot cannot end with the compromise in which right plea-bargains with wrong. Melodramatic action, once begun, must be pressed to clear-cut conclusions, decisively ended once and for all. Evil will be punished in *this* world, not the hereafter. And there is no ending more uncompromising than the death of one's antagonist. In the police story, justice is indefinitely suspended, the decisive combat postponed, until that final, cathartic scene in which the hero's previous inability to "speak" the definitive reply to the criminal violence is suddenly cured. All barriers that prevented the cop from closing with his antagonist are now cleared away; the plot can now be cleansed of pollution. Desire is, at last, transformed into deed. In this moment of purifying violence, all the frustrations of the hero's plot are focused into a gun barrel, all the delays of justice exploded by a single righteous bullet into the body of the criminal.

One of the satisfactions of fictional experience is the sense of an ending. *Stories* can provide us with the clean conclusions so often denied in the untidy plots of our lives. As Kaminsky argued in *American Film Genres,* in times of cultural instability audiences may prefer the awful clarity of violent resolution in fiction to negotiated, compromised endings that bring peace without victory. Citizens who perceive ubiquitous disrespect for the law, who fear for their property, their lives, and the morals of their children may more easily identify with the cop who is both the potential victim of criminal violence and the embattled defender of bourgeois morality. The feeling that one is essentially impotent, unable to control the direction of society or improve one's position within that society, may promote an appetite for melodrama. In the melodramatic universe, one can at least come to grips with the antagonist, confront the enemy face to face. Those who fear that the Vietnam experience, the hostage crisis in Iran, the situations in Lebanon and Nicaragua, and other blows to U.S. prestige have signaled national impotence may yearn for the violent moment of truth as an end to the agony of hesitation, indecision. Through an act of violence or the vicarious experience of such an act, a person can become fully committed in body and soul. In violence, *idea is action*. The split between mind and body is suddenly healed. When violence unifies a man (or a society) in a hot rush of single-minded purpose, the emotion one feels is pure, unmixed with doubt. Anthropologists and sports commentators agree that spectacles of ritualized violence (football, boxing, the bullfight, ritual sacrifice) can unite a community of partisan witnesses, can forge the sense of common identity so often lacking in a society composed of individual, frustrated destinies.

Those who wish to purge violence from media fiction should first consider why spectators want to witness violent action and why, if given the choice, they prefer a melodramatic universe to a tragic one. Rather than blindly fearing violence in television, we should understand it as a condensation and displacement of both public and private experience, as both a relief from the irresolution of the live world and a purification of its chaos.

The police story drives inexorably toward a shoot-out on the streets precisely because physical violence resolves conflicts with a clarity that an exchange of words could never achieve. It is said that people "resort" to violence when communication fails, implying that violence is a negation of language. But, as Fiske and Hartley write in *Reading Television,* "violence is only, after all, the continuation of *language by other means*." Violence is still a form of communication. It may be convulsive communication, rooted in the irrational; but human reality is as much emotional as conceptual. In many moments of our lives, we feel words to be inadequate vehicles for the speech of emotions.

Violence does not merely translate, but *transforms* the word into material language. Violence quite literally (physically) *informs* people of one's point of view, if only through the deformation of the antagonist's face. Whether expressed by a fist, a bullet, or a nuclear missile, such drastic forms of information/deformation can resolve conflicts and order the social universe, sometimes more decisively than the speaker intended. "No conflict, no drama," said George Bernard Shaw. Violence is essential to the police story (and to most televised drama) precisely because it condenses abstract conflicts and makes them visible. Fiske and Hartley claim that television violence usually:

> enacts social, rather than personal relations; it takes place between personalized moralities (good *v.* bad, efficient *v.* inefficient, culturally esteemed *v.* culturally deviant) rather than between individual people *per se*. There is perhaps no more economical and visually arresting way of enacting social conflicts which are in essence abstract and located in the mind than by means of an enacted slugging match. . . .

With many other communication theorists, Fiske and Hartley believe that viewing televised violence does not cause violent behavior in "real life" because viewers recognize that the "Police Story" shoot-out is a schematized fictional event, both framed off from reality and heavily conventionalized. They point out that the type of violence encountered on the screen is rarely faced by the individual viewer. "Real" violence normally occurs between two people who know each other well, such as husband and wife. But, with rare exceptions, violence on television comes from another—a stranger outside the bounds of family or friendship. Yet, it is exactly the spectacle of the violent stranger that leads some researchers to worry about the long-term effects of televised violence. Comparison of actual crime statistics with the number of violent crimes on television (in both news and fiction) shows that the world of television is far more violent than the reality most people live. But because television is *part* of the familiar lived world (*lebenswelt*) and because it is consciously or unconsciously regarded as a "witness" to the reality outside the home, viewers tend to see the world in terms of their television experience. Studies directed by George Gerbner indicate that "heavy" viewers of television overestimate their chances of being the victims of violent crimes. Although exposure to TV violence apparently does not cause or trigger violent behavior in the more or less sane viewer, Gerbner suggests that one result of violent television is an increased *fear* among viewers—a heightened atmosphere of suspicion concerning strangers. Gerbner himself fears that the result of televised violence may be a public demand for an authoritarian "law and order" society, with consequent risks to individual liberties.

—8—

Television Soap Opera: "Incest, Bigamy, and Fatal Disease"

by Charles Derry

To analyze soap opera is a difficult task, since one must first overcome the cultural prejudice against the genre. This prejudice is reflected even in the genre's name. The word *soap* is associated with these shows because originally they were used to sell soap and housekeeping products, as they still are. There is, therefore, irony and derision incorporated in the word. One cannot help but wonder why these shows came to be named for the products they sold. We do not refer to sports as beer or shaving shows, nor to the Saturday morning cartoons as breakfast food shows, nor to police shows like "The F.B.I." as automobile dramas. Associating these shows with the word *soap* implies that the genre is simply a vehicle to sell soap and, in and of itself, lacks any inherent meaning or value. Such an attitude indicates a prejudice in that it accuses one genre, the soap opera, of being what all television shows must be to their producers—that is, a means of selling a product.

More insidious is the male chauvinism in this attitude: the "soap" label binds these shows to that which our society has held to be unimportant: "women's work." This false association promotes the misguided, sexist premises that soap opera belongs exclusively to women and that the genre, therefore, reflects a sentimental, escapist, and/or hysterical sensibility. Studies of soap opera audiences have shown that the majority are women, in part because women have historically tended to be home in the afternoons when these programs are run; however, of the male television population at home in the afternoon, basically similar percentages are watching. High numbers of policemen, second-shift factory workers, and college students watch the soap opera as well—a fact that should effectively destroy the myth that their audiences are exclusively composed of unliberated housewives.

A sustained examination of soap opera reveals a sensibility that is nowhere Pollyanna-ish or simplistic but often ambiguous and ideologically progressive. The word *soap* further ties in to the genre's subversive subtext. There is an ironic symbiosis between the genre's "unwholesome" content, which deals with socially dirty or taboo concepts, and the commercials, which deal with thc superficial cleaning of surfaces. In this sense, the term *soap* redeems the program material by symbolically cleansing it. If Westerns are titled thus because they deal with the West, and detective shows titled thus because they deal with detectives, could our society really accept a genre entitled "Incest, Bigamy, and Fatal Disease"?

Like *soap*, the word *opera* tends to be derisive and ironic. Opera is high art which stylizes human emotional experience, while these programs are low art.

Opera is popularly disliked but respected, while television soap opera is popularly liked but disrespected. Thus, opera and, by extension, its audience are validated, while television soap opera and its audience are not. The *opera* appellation is nonironically relevant, however, in the way that the television soap opera, like its higher-art counterpart, is predicated upon extensive stylization of human emotional experience. Thus *soap* and *opera* both describe and ridicule the form. This cultural rejection of soap opera creates a situation of guilt for the viewers, who generally apologize for their pleasure. It is no wonder that soap opera producers and writers often call their product "daytime drama" to avoid such prejudicial baggage.

Until recently, the few critics who have deigned to look at television soap opera have overemphasized the genre's "therapeutic" effect on the viewer. The standard line of this argument is a familiar one: that soap operas fulfill the psychological need of the housewife who is bored by her role and who wants to feel that her own problems are minor in comparison to those of the soap opera characters. This viewpoint is ultimately simplistic, hardly encompassing enough to explain the more pervasive appeal of the afternoon soap opera, let alone the more culturally accepted (i.e., with a larger male audience) evening soap operas like "Dallas" or "Dynasty"; more seriously, it denies the possibility that the afternoon TV watchers actually are able to respond to these shows as artistic/mythic works. This is not to deny, of course, that some therapeutic effect is not operative; we simply assert that soap opera, like other genres, works within a more profound cultural perspective that both includes and transcends its specific and immediate psychological effect on the individual viewer.

Some critics fall into a different trap: a peremptory and generally pejorative categorization of all soap operas into one nebulous and static entity, which inherently disallows the existence of individual variation or evolution. Although obviously, as this very chapter suggests, it is useful to discuss soap operas together, there is inevitably a limit to the usefulness of the resultant generalizations, particularly if evaluatively invoked. Within the general category of soap opera exist a variety of individual works, each reflecting slightly different values and working toward slightly different ends. Just as Westerns reflect differences (for instance, a John Ford/John Wayne film like *The Searchers* endorses Christian civilization and manifest destiny, while an Arthur Penn/Dustin Hoffman film like *Little Big Man* rejects Christian civilization and manifest destiny), so too do soap operas—without eschewing their characteristic, shared structures—reflect differences. And yet critics rarely attempt to contrast different soap operas. What this simplistic viewpoint actually does is to emphasize pejoratively the inherent standardization of all generic works, and to suggest, in a subtle, dismissive way, that the standardization in soap opera is significantly more pervasive than in other genres. This fallacious and dangerous argument requires vociferous rejection because it has, at its roots, a rejection of a basic premise of genre theory itself: that is, the value of repetition in popular culture and the attendant dialectic involving standardization, variation, and artistry.

Other critics have mercilessly attacked soap opera for its "nonrealistic," melodramatic aspects. Certainly there are overwhelming problems with any aesthetic based on the concept of realism, since individuals have different conceptions as to what is or is not "realistic" based upon that which is congruent to their own unique experiences. This argument is itself a straw man, put forward to rationalize the prejudice against soap opera. Other generic works (for example, "Baretta" or "Kojak") are rarely criticized for their lack of reality, perhaps because their emphasis on a certain kind of content (in these examples, crime in the streets) seems to mitigate the stylization inherent in their own generic structures. If the soap opera seems somehow less "realistic," it may be because this genre refuses to hide the fact that it is presenting us with an unabashedly stylized view of the world: the popularity of the genre attests to the significance of the presented world view and gives the soap opera a relevance and mythic ritual that transcends any parochial or subjective considerations of realism.

Yet ironically, although on the obvious and manipulative level relating to plot irony, soap operas are not at all "real," on a more subtle level relating to the very structure of the genre, they are. One could argue that, as a result of the continuing nature of the tale, no other genre reflects a more pervasive isomorphism to certain qualities of real life than the soap opera. Historically, soap operas tend to be broadcast five days a week. The episodes are continuous—with Tuesday's show continuing where Monday's left off, and so forth. Even more crucial, however, is that at no point in the narrative is an ending to the tale predestined. In a traditional tragedy like *Oedipus,* for instance, we know that Oedipus will be brought down two hours or so after the beginning of the narrative; in a film like *Rocky*, we may not know whether Rocky will succeed in beating Apollo Creed, but we do know that his success or failure will not be determined until the end of the last reel. There is no parallel in the soap opera, since unless or until a series is cancelled, the narrative eschews any predetermined length. Soap operas have wildly differing life spans: "Hidden Faces," for instance, lasted only a few months, whereas "The Guiding Light" (on radio and television) has lasted over forty years.

Soap operas reject the traditionally structured plot, whereby a character is embroiled in a conflict that leads to an integrated series of crises and one concluding climax. Stories in soap opera move more with the haphazardness of life. Conflicts may develop quickly and then suddenly be suspended (in soap opera parlance, be "put on the back burner"); characters' problems may be solved haphazardly without a climax; a character may dominate the narrative and then suddenly become irrelevant. Sometimes a major event (such as a storm or a revealed secret) can, without warning, change everything. Other times, a main character, perhaps even one around whom an entire show is built, can suddenly die, and the narrative can simply and cruelly continue on—a shocking resilience relating to the real-life situation in which we all inevitably consider ourselves the focus of the primary narrative and find it difficult to conceive of a world going on without us. That some of these phenomena are caused, inevitably, by the exigencies of performers' contracts and ratings does not mitigate the basic, inescapable resemblances between soap opera and life: In both, things just keep happening. . . .

A good example of this unconventional narrative can be found in "All My Children," which dealt with the story of innocent Mary Kennicott, all-American girl, and her marriage to upstanding Dr. Jeff Martin, all-American boy. The problem began when Mary started to suffer dizzy spells. Although blood tests initially proved negative, the spells did not go away, and ultimately, the tests indicated a problem with Mary's blood cells. At least a year of episodes chronicled—albeit torturously slowly, on the back burner—Mary's health problem. The experienced viewer knew—indeed, at Mary's final fainting spell—that it was only a matter of time before the diagnosis would come in as . . . leukemia, and the story would jump to the front burner. One day, when Mary was at home and the audience was expecting the definitive lab results that would finally catapult the story to its inevitable hospital stay, pain, remission, remorse, regret, pregnancy, miscarriage, loss, and life-and-death struggle, an escaped convict broke into Mary's house and killed her. The leukemia story, so carefully set up, was itself aborted by the intruder who seemed almost outside the control of the writers themselves. In what other genre—other than life itself—is the precipitous removal of main characters such a seminal organizing principle? Thus the continuing nature of soap operas allows them to deal with the very capriciousness of existence.

If soap opera thus reflects an isomorphism with reality, it unarguably veers from reality in terms of the stylized way it organizes and presents its content. To understand exactly how soap opera is organized, it is useful to divide the genre into its component parts—focusing on temporal structures, spatial structures, themes, plots, and character types.

Temporal Structures

The temporal components of soap operas are extremely complex, in that contradictory time schemes can coexist. First there is what can be termed a *Landmark Time*: that is, the episode broadcast on Thanksgiving is generally represented as Thanksgiving, as is the Christmas episode Christmas. Landmark Time is complicated by the intrusion of *Extended Time*, whereby one day of soap opera story can be extended into a week or more of half-hour or hour episodes. Once on "General Hospital," preceding the murder of Phil Brewer, the show's chief villain for over ten years, one day of soap opera story took close to two months of episodes, and the hour including his murder took two weeks. Thus, it is possible for a soap opera to present a year of Landmark Time between Christmas episodes, even though, in Extended Time, the soap opera—in those approximately 250 episodes of story—presents only two or three weeks.

Occasionally, Extended Time and Landmark Time will conflict, resulting in an ellipsis. Once on "All My Children," the characters started, on a late June episode, to plan a Fourth of July celebration presumably to take place on the Fourth of July episode; consequently, many stories were thrust onto the front burner in ostensible preparation for potential crises on the picnic day. So much plot advancement was required for the writers that the June preparation extended beyond the Fourth of July episode. Thus, while the picnic was planned on one June morning on a late June episode, when the next morning came around, on an episode broadcast July 6 or 7, the characters found themselves discussing a Fourth of July that had already taken place and that had, of course, never been shown.

Soap opera time is also made more complicated by certain story events which are allowed their own idiosyncratic time schemes. For instance, although a woman may conceive on a November episode, she may not give birth until almost two years of episodes later; although the term of her pregnancy represents nine months, by the time of her delivery she may have actually passed two Christmas episodes pregnant (although by the same token, those episodes may have only represented four or five months of Extended Time). If pregnancy seems to take more time, early childhood growth seems to take less. If a soap opera girl is born, say, on a January episode, it is not at all surprising that on the episode broadcast exactly two years later, she (with the help of a different performer) may celebrate her fourth or fifth birthday. Similarly, a child may advance to teenage status in a matter of six or seven years. The benefit of this rapid growth is that once a child reaches the teens, she or he is qualified for sexual/romantic/familial problems; subsequently, children in soap opera grow so fast that members of different generations tend to be near contemporaries, and relatively young women tend to be grandparents even while continuing to have children of their own. Since prepubescent children tend not to be able to have soap-operatic problems, it is for these ages that the mortality rate is the highest. If a soap opera child can survive these years, she or he is lucky indeed: more often than not, survival can be attributed to the mercy and acumen of writers who will send the child into an upstairs room or boarding school for a few years or so, to be rescued at a useful older age when it is narratively convenient and not inordinately farfetched to do so.

The complexity of these time schemes is not problematic for the viewer, who easily follows the action, although it can be for the soap opera characters who are so obsessed by past events or consumed by their attempt to achieve some perfect future that they cannot attend properly to the present. More time confusions are created by typical narrative situations, whereby a character can have the same event transpire over and over—so that Diana on "General Hospital" can be periodically left husbandless with child, and Phil on "All My Children" can be several times reported missing and presumed dead, and the marriage plans of Frank and Jill on "Ryan's Hope" can be foiled by the successive intrusions of, so far, at least five "outsiders." Although time is continuous, the similarity of the future to the past makes time seem to double and triple back upon itself, potentially trapping the characters in Sisyphean destinies.

Spatial Structures

The spatial component of virtually every soap opera operates primarily within the context of a specific city—generally Smalltown, U.S.A. "All My Children" takes place in Pine Valley; "Another World" in Bay City; "General Hospital" in Port Charles; "Mary Hartman, Mary Hartman" in Fernwood; "Days of Our Lives" in Salem; and "As the World Turns" in Oakdale. So important is the city that it occasionally becomes the title of the show, as in "Somerset" and "Peyton Place." The big-city-based "Ryan's Hope," the ostensible exception, is (and not insignificantly) the most hermetic of soap operas, with a strikingly small primary cast; indeed, its location is not Manhattan as much as it is Maeve Ryan's kitchen around which the small inbred Riverside community congregates. Fictional soap opera cities are often given elaborate geographical identities. Pine Valley, for instance, is close

Kim Delaney and Laurence Lau in "All My Children."

Gloria De Haven and Cali Timmins in "Ryan's Hope."

James Kibard and Calla White in "Loving."

enough to commute to New York City by train; two of its neighbor cities include Center City (which is where the prostitutes live) and Llanview, Pennsylvania, the base of operations for "One Life to Live." The proximity of Llanview, Pennsylvania (as well as its creation by Agnes Nixon, the writer-producer of "All My Children"), allows the soap operatic worlds of these two series to connect and enables characters to occasionally move from one show (and city) to the other—as attorney Paul Martin of "All My Children" did once for the murder trial of Vicki Riley of "One Life to Live," and a second time, years later, for the murder trial of Vicki's husband, Clint Buchanan.

The stability of the usual setting contrasts with the turbulence of the characters' personal lives. Soap opera towns are comprised of designer boutiques, designer hospitals, well-appointed homes in a variety of tasteful/conventional styles, and plenty of opportunities to accidentally run into your enemies at the health club/art gallery/free clinic/disco.

The incursion of political corruption or crime becomes therefore all the more horrifying. The mythically beleaguered town of Monticello, locale of "The Edge of Night," must deal with the seemingly unending horrors inflicted by psychotic killers and organized-crime chieftains; Llanview has had already to deal with its first massage parlor as well as with left-wing terrorism; the New York City of "Ryan's Hope" is riddled through and through with mob control, nursing home scandals, and political shenanigans. The most recurrent example of corruption in these programs is prostitution. Perhaps the title "The Edge of Night" provides the most apt metaphor: the nearness of darkness and decay to communities that appear to be light and forthright. If this metaphor emphasizes the corruption of our society, the metaphoric title of "The Secret Storm" emphasizes the corruption and obsessions of the individual.

The emphasis on the individual psyche in soap operas is reflected in the emphasis on the world of the indoors. Certainly the enclosed spaces of the soap opera contribute to a sense of entrapment, allowing the characters to contemplate, discuss, and act upon their guilty desires. Given this emphasis on interiors, it is not surprising that the soap opera has developed a stable of specific interiors—each of which serves a metaphorical function that allows the genre to deal with one or more of its themes.

Among the most important of these interiors is *The Hospital*, which is always, no matter how small a town, one of the most modern in the country, with the latest multimillion-dollar technological equipment. Its staff, however, includes only a few surgeons who are talented enough to do emergency surgery, a situation that inevitably causes problems when an emergency occurs while a surgeon has a broken arm or is temporarily psychologically paralyzed. This interior allows the genre to deal with the theme of life and death: patients hovering on the edges of existence, guilt-ridden, contemplative, their own destinies about to be sealed as ever-widening circles of cause and effect engulf the other characters and their world. Many soap operas emphasize the hospital almost exclusively—an emphasis reflected in titles such as "The Nurses," "The Doctors," and "General Hospital." Indeed, there is no afternoon soap opera that does not include a hospital in a more or less prominent position.

The Court Room serves the genre as a locale where characters can deal with right and wrong, guilt and innocence. Inevitably, a major story will build to a murder and then culminate in a dramatic trial in which culpability will be attributed. Guilt in soap operas is complex: generally, whenever a murder is committed, most of the characters are psychologically guilty of having at least wished the evil deed. Uncovering the actual murderer—who is often psychologically innocent—is quite difficult. Significantly, the use of the courtroom does not reflect the genre's faith in social justice or the American political system. On the contrary, the soap opera suggests that justice cannot be organized by a social agency but only, on occasion, by a capricious fate. The government frequently puts the wrong party on trial, just as the jury almost always finds the innocent person guilty.

On "All My Children," Kelly Cole found herself on death row, saved at the last moment when an automobile accident caused Claudette Montgomery to make a deathbed confession. Jessie Brewer of "General Hospital" has gone to jail for at least two murders she did not commit; the helpless policemen on that show arrested at least three innocent people for the murder of Phil Brewer before they got it right. Murder trials do at least promote moral discernments and the opportunity for truth to out. On the witness stand, characters reveal secrets—dark and hidden for years—and pay emotionally for every past sin. Guilt, humiliation, retribution, punishment, purgation, and exoneration exist in a complex dynamic that envelops all the characters in the community. Although the lawyers may not be responsible for the ultimate propagation of justice, soap opera characters naively refuse to lose faith in the system and, Candide-like, offer reassurances to each other in the midst of calamity, inequity, and woe.

The Newspaper Office and The TV Studio function as a place for the dissemination of information or gossip, thus documenting the dynamic by which the attitudes and sensibilities of the soap opera community are formed. There is or was a newspaper office in "Peyton Place," "Somerset," "One Life to Live," and "The Edge of Night," among others. There is or was a television studio in "Ryan's Hope," "One Life to Live," "General Hospital," and "All My Children." Many of soap opera's most attractive characters are involved in the media search for truth: the late Joe Riley, editor extraordinaire of "One Life to Live," for instance, or Jack Fenelli, hard-hitting columnist of "Ryan's Hope." Of all the soap operas, "Mary Hartman, Mary Hartman" took fullest advantage of these themes, making obsessive fun of media targets as varied as Dinah Shore, David Susskind, cinema vérité, the eleven o'clock news, the television talk show, the radio call-in program, and investigative reporting—in the process lambasting the media's role in programming us to bourgeois tastes and attitudes. "Mary Hartman, Mary Hartman" is in contrast, of course, to the more conventional soap opera, which often presents the media as having an almost mystical relationship with truth and discovery.

The Restaurant or Nightclub allows the genre to deal with the process of socialization. In these locations people meet, glances are exchanged, trysts are arranged, coincidences occur, secrets are overheard, and rumors are begun. If the soap opera generally eschews exteriors, it is the nightclub that provides an interior to which the characters can journey in search of human contact or social reinforcement. Not surprisingly, encounters are frequently disastrous. Recently, the soaps have been coming to terms with the Me Decade: Conventional meeting places like the Chateau Restaurant in "All My Children" or the work cafeteria in "Mary Hartman, Mary Hartman" are being joined by more narcissistic interiors such as the disco in "General Hospital" and the health club in "One Life to Live," the latter allowing the characters to intermingle traumatically in various stages of natural, athletic undress.

Lastly, *The Private Home* provides the setting for the most personal obsessions of the individual: the ambitions, dreams, guilts, and sexual pleasures that originate here, only to affect/contaminate/transform the entire community. Until the last few years, the emphasis has been on the sitting or living room: sipping coffee or tea, characters would talk to each other about their problems. More recently, however, the bedroom has increasingly become a major focus: no longer do we only hear characters talking about their sexual/romantic exploits, we witness them (albeit tastefully, with careful ellipses and only marginal nudity). Although "Mary Hartman, Mary Hartman" set many of its intimate scenes in Mary's bedroom, this show in large part rejected the sitting room in its feminist quest for social criticism. Imprisoning Mary instead in her kitchen, dooming her to endless coffee making and floor polishing, the room so completely defined her existence that it was here that Mary held the funeral for her next-door neighbor who had drowned in a bowl of Mary's soup.

Conventional Themes

The third component of soap opera, the thematic, is best approached through a trichotomous organization: (1) the breaking of taboos, (2) the basic horrific and random destiny, which organizes the universe and all of our lives, and (3) the twin mysteries of birth and death, which confront and confound us at every turn.

In *Totem and Taboo,* Freud discusses one of the most basic taboos: the prohibition against having sexual intercourse with members of forbidden totem clans. Just what constitutes a taboo varies among cultures, but soap operas most frequently present a dominant female character who breaks the taboos defined by the status quo—either consciously or as a result of subconscious urges she can neither understand nor control. Invariably, this female is one of the most popular characters on the program. Although she may be committing acts society would regard as destructive, our attitude towards her is ambivalent and rather sympathetic. She does what others refrain from because they fear the social disruption and personal tragedy that may result from breaking the taboo.

After undergoing two miserable marriages, unhappy, doomed Erica on "All My Children" finally finds a man whom she loves and who loves her; we empathize with her determination to marry him, although we are taken aback at the revelation—discovered but not believed by Erica until the last moment—that the man she intends to marry is actually a long-lost half-brother. Narrowly escaping that taboo, Erica's fixation on her dead father leads her next to an erotic obsession with Nick Davis, the older man who had been the best friend of Erica's own mother as well as the father of one of Erica's own ex-husbands. Incestuous and pseudo-incestuous relationships like these are common. Another example can be found in "Ryan's Hope," whose main empathetic villain Delia Reed—herself denied as a child the comfort of a secure nuclear family—has been working consistently to attach herself to any one of the male members of the Ryan family. Delia first fell in love with Pat Ryan, shortly thereafter married his older brother Frank Ryan, pushed Frank down the stairs when she discovered he was having an affair with Jillian Coleridge, divorced Frank and through trickery managed to marry Pat Ryan, who developed a drug problem and eventually extricated himself from the marriage in order to develop a relationship with Jillian Coleridge's sister Faith. As of 1980, Delia had married and divorced Roger Coleridge (brother to Jillian and Faith) and was introducing herself as Delia Reed Ryan Ryan Coleridge even while working on a romance with Barry Ryan, a cousin from Chicago imported expressly, it would seem, so yet another Ryan could potentially participate in the ongoing breaking of taboos by the doomed heroine, who eventually ran Barry over with a car.

Anyone who violates a taboo and challenges society can then become taboo and infect others. Erica on "All My Children," for instance, has at times been avoided like the plague by almost everyone in Pine Valley. Occasionally "All My Children" will present an episode comprised of good-intentioned Erica making calls on a variety of characters, all of whose lives she obliviously leaves in shambles.

The contagion of the taboo breaker is itself a kind of punishment which ensures that taboo-breaking is not condoned. Although we may wish that the taboo breaker be punished, our response is complex, because we spend so much time in secret empathy that our hope is eventually replaced by a dread of the inevitable outcome. Often sins and deceit will so compound themselves in the course of several years of a soap opera narrative that no punishment could ever redress the broken taboos. The genre rejects any simple concepts of justice and rarely punishes the taboo breaker at the moment of his or her most arrogant act. What happens more frequently is that circumstances begin to change the behavior of the taboo breaker—who is not punished until her or his life has already begun to become more conventional. Thus, when the punishment arrives, there is the overwhelming sense that it is no longer fair. Even worse, the punishment often destroys the former taboo breaker, who becomes contaminated once again.

A recent example of this can be found in Karen Wolek's adventures on "One Life to Live." Karen began as the archetypal evil woman. Mean and petty toward her sister, Jenny, an ex-nun, the ex-con Karen schemed herself into marriage with a respectable doctor and then promptly became a nymphomaniac and a prostitute. Her sordid life climaxed with a hit-and-run accident which left a little boy dead and at least three lives shattered. The virtuous heroine Vicki came to Karen's aid and helped Karen change her ways; just as Karen was almost completely transformed, fate intervened again and put Vicki on trial for murder. Only Karen's testimony could help clear her; it was, dramatically, during cross-examination that Karen's overwhelming guilt was expiated in a remarkable courtroom scene in which Karen, in a selfless attempt to save Vicki, allowed herself to be broken down, hysterically confessing her nymphomania, prostitution, and manslaughter to a shocked town. So completely destroyed and humiliated was Karen that the audience could not help but feel guilty for having ever wished Karen's sins to be revealed. Karen spent the subsequent year of the story undergoing more trials, redeemed by her suffering and assimilated back into Llanview society only when she was victimized and raped by her taboo-breaking brother-in-law.

If villainous women like Karen are often redeemed (if temporarily), villainous men are often simply expelled from the soap opera community. Sometimes they are killed—which results in a trial and untold misery for the other characters; other times they merely go away—to Argentina or somewhere, coming back periodically to do more damage when the plot requires stirring. In the last few years, however, there have been a variety of villainous men, who, in their own neurotic ways, break taboos, are redeemed, and break taboos again—much like the villainous women. Perhaps the best example is the dashing ex-tennis pro Brad Vernon, also from "One Life to Live." That men like Brad Vernon can now be ambivalent villains who secure audience empathy seems symptomatic of some liberating quality in recent soap opera, some tacit (if unconscious) validation that the issues soap opera deals with are of interest, not only to housewives, but to us all.

Soap operas do not, however, as is sometimes claimed, deal simplistically with the idea of sin being followed inexorably by punishment. Although it is true that taboo breakers are generally punished, it is also true that those who do not break taboos are also generally punished—though for what? If many plots revolve around an individual transgressing society's rules, just as many revolve around a conventional individual buffeted by an essentially horrific destiny. A good person will be struck by a train and develop amnesia (Donna Beck Tyler on "All My Children"); a doctor, on the verge of announcing the solution to a mystery, will suddenly have a heart attack and die (Dr. Peter Taylor on "General Hospital"); a virtuous heroine will be viciously killed by thugs (Mary Ryan on "Ryan's Hope"). The innocent, you see, suffer also.

Indeed, perhaps the most important aspect of soap opera is the way the genre reflects some of our most profound fears: that is, that the universe is hostile, that fate conspires against us, that every life leads inevitably to death. If our belief in God or a plan allows that hubris will be punished by nemesis, our skepticism regarding God's goodness allows that innocence will also be punished. No one stays happy. ("Therefore," chants the chorus in *Oedipus,* "while our eyes wait to see the destined final day, we must call no one happy who is of mortal race, until he hath crossed life's border, free from pain.") Our empathy with the taboo breaker stems directly from this cynicism: if one cannot count on just rewards, why should one accept moral constraints? Why not pursue fulfillment according to one's own selfish instincts?

So obsessively willed is selfish Erica on "All My Children" that every one of her successful plots represents a minor victory over the chaotic and malevolent destiny. It is this emphasis on *destiny* that is responsible for the major mode of irony that the soap opera so clearly expresses. Two examples will suffice. The first ten years of "General Hospital" revolved around the doomed love affair between Dr. Steve Hardy and Audrey March. A variety of problems kept them irrevocably apart, love-torn and unhappy. When finally, after a decade of episodes, a nonchalant conversation turned suddenly into a mutual declaration of love, Dr. Hardy (goodness personified) announced to Audrey, "We're going to live happily ever after," and bounded ecstatically out of the room, whereupon he promptly fell down a flight of stairs and became critically injured. Only soap opera could get away with that kind of blatantly ironic and bleak juxtaposition. Likewise, a character may cause misery for others even though she or he is not, strictly speaking, a taboo breaker. A good example of this is Jennie, the virtuous ex-nun from "One Life to Live," whom fate seems to take an extra pleasure in torturing. Pursued at various times by at least four different men, Jennie saw the first die in a fall during an argument in which he was trying to convince others that he wasn't corrupting her; the second guiltily give up his romantic obsession with Jennie when his jealous wife committed suicide; the third become a rapist, a corporate criminal, and possibly a murderer; and the fourth institutionalize his jealousy-crazed wife and then himself die in a horrible automobile accident while trying to prevent Jennie from hearing a life-shattering secret. Jennie is a kind of taboo but not a taboo breaker: suffering, smiling, blameless, innocent, beloved—but with fate dooming her and those around her to cosmic unhappiness.

Accompanying soap opera's emphasis on taboos and fate is the genre's obsession with the twin mysteries of birth and death. Women in soap opera are always obsessed with pregnancy: will they deliver safely? Time is most extended during the nine months in which the woman carries her child; has there ever been even one soap opera pregnancy that did not include a hospital stay after a near miscarriage? If it is the mother who is given the responsibility of childbirth (always portrayed as dangerous, traumatic, but wished for), it is the father who is given the responsibility for the actual genesis of life—but which man?

Paternity is soap opera's most critical and often unknowable issue. Little Phil Tyler's father on "All My Children" is not Chuck Tyler but actually Phil Brent; similarly, Phil Brent's own father is not Ted Brent but Nick Davis. Little Brian Kendall's father on "One Life to Live" is not Paul Kendall but actually Tony Harris; similarly, Tony's father is actually the multimillionaire Victor Lord, whose name Tony finally adopts. Soap operas can be seen as a search for paternity, an exploration of the meaning of the man/woman union in the face of their different physiological relationship to the procreative function. It is not at all uncommon for a soap opera to reveal or alter a paternity long after a child's birth. Although "General Hospital" began in 1963, only several years ago was Dr. Steve Hardy revealed to be the father of Dr. Jeff Webber. An excellent example of the typical paternity confusion occurred in recent years on "Ryan's Hope," where a pregnant Jillian was to marry Frank Ryan, the love of her life. Unfortunately, Jill's happiness disappeared when blood tests revealed that the father was actually Seneca Beaulac. Only after she married Seneca did further tests show that the baby was actually Frank Ryan's in the first place. Had not fate intervened and killed the child, the writers of "Ryan's Hope" might have decided years from now that the father was, once again,

Seneca. Instead they decided to revise Jill's own paternity, surprisingly revealing that Jill's adoptive father, Ed Coleridge, dead already for over five years, was in actuality Jill's birth father as well.

The soap opera emphasis on the prebirth state and the attendant concerns of miscarriage, stillbirth, and abortion are balanced by the genre's emphasis on the predeath state of semiconsciousness and coma and the attendant concerns of mercy killing and suicide. At what point does an individual really die? Soap opera characters constantly fall into critical comas, as they linger for months of episodes in semiconscious states. And yet even when a character does die, this finality is attenuated by the fact that, as often as not, he or she comes back! In soap opera you can never count on a character's death—particularly if you haven't seen the body in the casket. And even if you have (for instance, Marco Dane in "One Life to Live"), it's possible that the individual may return (you see, the real corpse was Mario Dane, Marco's twin brother, invented specifically by the writers to allow Marco's complex return). Phil Brent on "All My Children" has already returned once from the dead and, although currently deceased, he has more than an even chance of returning again.

As with procreation, the ambiguity regarding mortality tends to be more often reserved for men. It is almost as if man's mobility, unhampered by pregnancy and its complications, inherently allows him the facility to transcend physical limits more easily. Women are invariably victims of this ambiguity, forced into accidental bigamy upon the return of their presumed-dead spouses. Ironically, both these birth and death concerns tend to put women in the victim position, a circumstance that understandably promotes feminist analysis of the genre.

Conventional Plots

In the service of the thematic organizations articulated above, the soap opera enlists a variety of conventional plots. They are described below.

Love Confronted by Obstacles

Soap operas thrive on the love affair that cannot be consummated. Perhaps the best example—certainly the most drawn out—is the story of Phil and Tara on "All My Children." Although they loved each other as far back as high school, their marriage plans fell through when Phil left town after he developed amnesia upon the discovery of his real parentage. In the meantime, Tara became involved with Phil's best friend Chuck and indeed would have married him had he not, in the middle of the ceremony, gone into kidney failure. While Chuck recuperated, the returned Phil, himself recovered, reestablished his relationship with Tara. As Tara decided to break it off with Chuck, Phil was unexpectedly drafted. A snowstorm on the eve of Phil's departure overseas prevented their elopement, so Tara and Phil married themselves in a makeshift ceremony. Just as Chuck had recovered enough to allow Tara to tell him the truth about her relationship with Phil, word came that Phil had been killed in Vietnam. Tara decided to go through with the wedding to Chuck—because now she was carrying Phil's child, which needed a father. Surprisingly, miraculously, Phil came back from Vietnam—not really dead—and figured out, after more than a year, that Tara's child was really his, but not before he married Erica out of desperation and loneliness. Remembering how Phil reacted to the revelation of his own paternity, Tara was too afraid to disrupt her own marriage and reveal her son's actual paternity—even though she still loved Phil. By the time Phil divorced Erica, Tara was finally psychologically ready to leave Chuck. Just as she was about to tell Chuck that she wanted to marry her one great love, Chuck went into kidney failure—again postponing the inevitable. By the time Chuck was sufficiently recovered to be told of Tara's and Phil's intentions, Phil's son, who did not yet know who his real father was, had begun opposing his mother's divorce and developing psychosomatic asthma attacks which were successfully preventing his parent's union. When Tara and Phil finally did get together—many obstacles later—Phil was transferred to Washington, where he promptly went on a secret mission and was reported killed. Tara moved back to Pine Valley, where she was cautiously being comforted by Chuck, who had since himself remarried. . . .

The Slow and Drawn-Out Death

Shall the plugs be pulled? Can one die in dignity? Occasionally, when a romance does manage to succeed against all obstacles, and when the audience will not allow the writers to give the characters any more problems that will pit them against one another, the only solution is to give one of the characters an incurable disease. This is precisely what happened to Linc Tyler and the late Kitty Shea on "All My Children." So popular was this story that the actress who played Kitty was resurrected as Kitty's long-lost twin sister Kelly, who then proceeded to fall in love with Linc Tyler herself.

The Sudden and Unexpected Accident or Illiness

This device seems always to work as a reminder that fate can intercede at any moment and dramatically, in one bold stroke, change everything. Examples include Brian's accident on "One Life to Live" or Mary Ryan's death on "Ryan's Hope."

Personal Tensions That Erupt into a Murder and a Trial

This plot is used periodically by almost every soap opera. Examples include the murder of Eddie Dorrance on "All My Children" and the murder of Marco (or was it Mario?) on "One Life to Live."

The Intrusion of a Psychotic Killer

When events are not complex enough in themselves, the writers can introduce a psychotic killer. In "Ryan's Hope," for instance, there was Kenneth Castle, who terrorized Faith Coleridge before pushing her father off a roof.

The Appearance of the Split Personality

This plot twist raises the issue of identity, wherein a good character is threatened by a second personality over which he or she has little control. In "One Life to Live," for instance, Kathy Craig escaped her problems by escaping into the identity of Kitty Mainwaring. Similarly, in the same show, virtuous Vicki Riley has been occasionally taken over by her alter ego Nicki Smith.

The Romeo and Juliet Story

Often a romance blossoms between characters of different backgrounds. Examples include rich Linc Tyler and poor Kitty Shea of "All My Children," Irish Eileen Riley and Jewish David Siegel of "One Life to Live," and the middle-aged Ellen Grant and very young Dale Robinson of "Somerset."

Amnesia

At the drop of a hat, characters can suffer memory loss, a condition that usually serves to convolute time by effectively undoing large portions of the narrative. A good example is from "All My Children," where Donna Beck, a hardened prostitute, spent almost two years of episodes changing into an innocent, reformed young wife. Just as the transformation became complete, a train accident triggered amnesia; when Donna regained consciousness, she thought she was still a prostitute, and the entire process of evolution and transformation had to begin all over again.

Unintentional Bigamy

The most famous soap opera bigamists include Jessie Brewer Taylor of "General Hospital," who was married to Peter Taylor as well as to Phil Brewer; her friend Audrey Baldwin Hardy, who was married to Steve Hardy as well as to Tom Baldwin; and Vicki Burke Riley of "One Life to Live," who was married to Steven Burke and Joe Riley.

Career Strivings

Many soap operas revolve around a company and the various characters who try to get ahead: examples include the Delaney Brands Company in "Somerset," Ewing Oil in "Dallas," and the Frame Enterprises in "Another World." Increasingly, women are insisting on careers too: Nina as a corporate executive in "All My Children," Loretta as a country-western singer on "Mary Hartman, Mary Hartman."

Romantic and Sexual Adventures

The most obvious (and often convoluted) of the conventional soap opera plots concern love and sex. On "General Hospital," for instance, Diana loved Phil, who loved Jessie, who was married to Peter, who offered to marry Diana, who was much later jealous of Leslie, who loved Rick, who loved Monica, who was married to Jeff, who became enamored of Diana . . . and so forth. Human companionship is valuable and difficult to attain; certainly an irony of soap opera is that the characters spend so much of their time chasing after fulfillment with so little success.

Character Types

Characterization and types, comprising the final component of soap opera, tend to be subordinated to plot. Striking in soap opera is the way that characters are isolated from any contemporary context. References to real news are extremely rare; current events are introduced only when they can be used as plot devices. Vietnam has been frequently invoked, but usually not as a social or political issue as much as a place from which characters could be missing in action. Soap opera characters do not read books; they do not go to movies; they do not talk about politics; they tend not to have hobbies; they tend not to watch television; and, except for weddings and funerals, they tend not to go to church—in short, when you put them in a room together, they have nothing else to talk about except whether or not they are happy.

Soap opera characters *are* their problems. This decultured context raises the soap opera to the level of myth. When the characters converse, as they do endlessly, it is invariably about tragedy. Because the stories are continuing, almost anything a character says has an ironic horrific subtext relating to some past trauma that has not yet been resolved. Characters imprison themselves in their own past: can they ever forget? Certainly they cannot learn—either from their own experiences or from the experiences of others. Characters generally exhibit a total obliviousness to the implications of the stories in which they are involved and the lessons they should be learning. A good example is from "All My Children," where a major plot line of its first decade revolved around the countless horrible repercussions of having suppressed Little Phil's true paternity. When the situation finally erupted into one overwhelming catastrophe, the character of Anne Tyler reflected on what a horrible decision had been made so many years ago in creating the lie and then blithely attempted, on that very episode, to arrange a similar deception in regard to her own unborn child. Soap opera characters are self-absorbed, clever, stupid, and doomed; like us?

Among the characters, there is, first of all, a distinction between *The Involved* and *The Uninvolved.* Characters in the former category are actively involved in trauma and adventure. Characters in the latter category, in soap opera parlance referred to as tent-pole characters, have few adventures, existing mainly so that the involved can have someone to talk to. The uninvolved keep the tent of the show standing, while the others thrash about within it. Jessie Brewer, on "General Hospital," began her soap opera career as one of the most active of the involved characters: for ten years she was intimate with murder, adultery, bigamy, and fatal disease. More recently, as new and younger characters have been introduced, Jessie has been transformed into a tent-pole character without significant problems. For weeks at a time, she may be almost completely written out of the action; when she does participate, it is generally to offer advice, warning, or sympathy. She and the once involved Dr. Steve Hardy of the same show have been transformed into a kind of matriarch and patriarch: fine parent figures, because they keep their advice good and themselves scarce. There is something comforting in this kind of transformation. Although it may reveal the character's inability to remain dramatic and retain the interest of the audience, it offers a rare respite from suffering. How nice that after ten years of misery, Jessie can now have some years of relative peace. Other tent-pole characters include Kate Martin in "All My Children," Maeve Ryan on "Ryan's Hope," and Will Vernon on "One Life to Live."

The involved characters can themselves be divided into *The Active* and *The Passive*—those who actively break taboos and suffer and those who passively allow fate (and others) to buffet them horrifically. Perhaps the archetypal examples of this dichotomy are Erica and Tara from "All My Children": Erica, the femme fatale, who refuses to allow anything to stand in her way, and Tara, a dishrag heroine, devoted to her child and to anyone with a problem. Each character represents an opposing response to soap opera's unanswering *Weltanschauung*.

Most of the characters on soap opera tend to be middle- or upper-middle-class. They gravitate toward the professions of doctor and lawyer. Other typical occupations include business, journalism, nursing, and writing. Soap operas present a world that is upwardly mobile. Although it is the doctors and lawyers who impress us, it is the working-class characters, trying to escape their class, who most provoke our empathy. Bobbi Spencer, for a while the most neurotic and empathetic villain of "General Hospital," is an orphan and former prostitute determined to succeed no matter what; becoming a nurse was only her first step. The same show's lower-class Heather at one point married for money and then sold her own baby to get ahead. Marco Dane of "One Life to Live," an eternal outsider, tried to succeed through pimping and organized crime; when these schemes failed, he simply adopted the identity of a doctor and went to work in the local hospital, the townspeople almost instantly according him respect because of his title.

Although many critics have objected to soap opera's depiction of the traditional women's roles as mother, daughter, and housewife, the fact remains that soap opera depicts more women with careers than does any other genre. Two leading characters on "General Hospital," Leslie Webber and Monica Webber Quartermaine, are both doctors;

on "One Life to Live," the main characters, Vicki Riley and Pat Ashley, are both journalists; and the Coleridge sisters of "Ryan's Hope," Faith and Jill, are, respectively, a doctor and an attorney extraordinaire. Rare is the soap opera female who doesn't also hold down a job outside the home.

Related to upward mobility and the bourgeois values such strivings reflect is the decidedly WASP identity of most soap opera characters. Pioneering work to transcend this orientation was done on Agnes Nixon's "One Life to Live," which introduced ethnic Jews, blacks, and Poles as major characters, as well as on "Ryan's Hope," with its aggressive working-class Irish-Catholic New York milieu and its ethnic Italians and Latinos. There is, nevertheless, a distinction on most soap operas between the upper-middle-class WASP and others; the latter tend to be more colorful and speak in working-class accents, which often seem to parody their class or heritage. Minorities are not always completely assimilated into the soap opera narrative; for example, although there are blacks on "All My Children," they remained tent-pole characters throughout the early years of the series; when, several years ago, Frank and Nancy did acquire a plot of their own, it tended to parallel rather than intersect those of other characters. Only in the last several years have the stories of black characters begun more strikingly to intermesh with the narrative as a whole.

Despite the fact that certain character types recur—such as the perfectly good woman (Jessie) or the all-forgiving, understanding man (the late Peter Taylor of "General Hospital")—soap opera characters are surprisingly three-dimensional. This is in part promoted by certain exigencies of soap opera production: (1) an established soap opera actor is often replaced by another actor to play the same character, (2) each actor, when playing the same role virtually every day for years, cannot help but bring to the performance some of her or his own actual personality, and (3) as writers are replaced, characters and their behavior cannot help but change. Thus while soap opera characters may be basically stock and subservient to the narrative, they become complex as they constantly exhibit paradoxical behavior which is then assimilated into our understanding of their characters.

Concluding Ideas

Of course, even within the generic structures outlined in this analysis, each soap opera inevitably expresses a different orientation or emphasis which should not be ignored. "All My Children," for instance, is among the soap operas most interested in topical subjects such as abortion, battered children, Vietnam, infant crib death, and drug use—subjects particularly exploited in its early years. It was "All My Children" that showed a real actress (Eileen Letchworth as Margo) undergoing an actual face-lift. The stories on this series tend often to be formally parallel and purposely repetitive.

"Ryan's Hope," in many ways atypical, constructs its narrative with only a few major characters and often replaces traditional soap opera melodrama with perceptive and revealing dialogue. If it is Phoebe Tyler's evil schemes against Kitty Shea that the audience remembered on "All My Children," it is, typically, Siobhan talking quietly to her mother about her unhappy childhood that the audience remembers on "Ryan's Hope." If other soap operas stress essentially horrific fate, "Ryan's Hope" humanistically stresses our capacity to endure and transcend.

"Somerset" was in many ways the most ritualized of the soap operas: it presented a self-contained town into which arrived new characters who would catalyze a plot and then (1) join the community, (2) leave town, (3) get killed, or (4) go insane and join the nether-community in the asylum outside of town. In the few years "Somerset" was on the air, it sent numerous women into the asylum: Kate, who came to town, fell in love with Julian, and left in a catatonic fit; Julian's former wife, Zoe, who was also driven crazy; Jerry's first wife; Rex Cooper's wife, Laura; and others. The hidden meaning of "Somerset" was certainly feminist in its implications: men drive women crazy.

"One Life to Live" is the most melodramatic, reflective, and almost deliriously excessive soap in its use of irony and contrivances; barely a week goes by without some character discussing in shell-shocked tones the malevolence of the universe and our subservience to fate.

"Mary Hartman, Mary Hartman" was, more than any other soap, the most self-conscious about its form, which it used to criticize the organization of American life and its inherent chauvinist, unhealthy premises. Television, for "Mary Hartman, Mary Hartman," was the great value-leveler, presenting images of the Vietnam war alongside those of Bugs Bunny, Lucille Ball, and toothpaste commercials. Thus the American woman is bombarded by messages from a variety of sources, none of them clearly more valuable or important than any of the others. In the opening episode of "Mary Hartman, Mary Hartman," Mary was sent word that a mad killer had killed the entire Lombardi family and their two goats and eight chickens. Mary's response—"What kind of madman would shoot two goats and eight chickens . . . and the people, of course, the people. . . ."—and her immediate attention to the waxy yellow buildup on her floor revealed her tragic and comic inability to make distinctions of value. "Mary Hartman, Mary Hartman" took what was excluded from all the other soap operas—that is, the American cultural context—and held it responsible for all of its characters' problems; structurally, the narrative replaced fate with America. By the end of the first season of episodes, Mary Hartman was reduced to catatonia in an insane asylum, bludgeoned to a peaceful respite by the combined force of Mr. Coffee coffee makers, her precocious daughter Heather, the six o'clock news, her husband's macho chauvinism, the anti-Semitism of Bible Belt Ohio, the welfare system, EST, and a disconnected crisis line.

A final, crucial point about soap opera concerns the way the generic material reaches the audience. Although soap operas are televised, it has been noted that audiences do not watch consistently from beginning to end the way they might watch a movie or even a "validated" program like "Hill Street Blues." Since many soap opera watchers are simultaneously cleaning house, studying, or eating, they do not always pay the kind of attention generally afforded other aesthetic creations. In fact, it is not at all unusual for an individual to listen to a soap opera from another room (without seeing the picture) or to watch the picture (with the sound turned off) while talking on the phone; that either the image or sound alone is often sufficient to communicate the genre's essence is testament to the high level of redundancy.

Clearly, the content is significantly more important than the specific form in which that content is embodied. This leads to a crucial fact: that is, it is possible to "watch" television soap opera without even owning a television set. The continuing stories are chronicled in numerous books, many magazines, and syndicated weekly soap opera columns in most big-city newspapers. There is, as well, an ongoing network of soap opera watchers who communicate with each other in person, by phone, and in letter as to the latest development. Many soap opera "watchers" are those who have literally watched the shows for a period of their lives and now continue to "watch" them through other means.

The ongoing adventures of Tara and Erica seep, by a kind of cultural osmosis, into our social and psychological world; the evil of J.R. has a meaning even for those who do not watch "Dallas" every week. Soap opera may be television's closest analogue to pure myth, where the created aesthetic experience is less important than the ongoing, hidden mythical structure. Future study of soap opera might well take Claude Levi-Strauss and structural anthropology as a model and view soap opera as revelatory of our contemporary beliefs and needs. Soap opera invites this kind of analysis—which will surely follow; and indeed, perhaps only then will soap opera achieve the respectability that it so clearly deserves.

part three
PSYCHOLOGICAL APPROACHES

Part three contains three specific applications of ideas taken from the eminent psychological theorists C. G. Jung, Sigmund Freud, and Erik Erikson. The limitation of the section is self-evident. It is not an exhaustive look at the application of all, many, or even one psychoanalytic model. We are also not saying that these three analysts are the prime, correct, or most important ones in the history of psychological thought.

What, in fact, we are doing here is taking three analytical positions that share some assumptions and disagree on others and showing how the individual ideas can be applied to specific television formulas. Once again, we are involved with presenting a model intended to teach us something about the specific kind of show being examined at the same time it presents some insights into a more general way of approaching the act of popular creation.

Freud's theories are very much ego based, centering on the assumed importance of the individual ego and the apparently necessary traumas each ego must face and with which it must deal. Applications of Freud therefore tend to be "I" oriented, informed by what they tell us about the direct relation of individuals to the experience under discussion, in this case television detectives. The television detective's adventures can even be seen as popular parallels to the process of psychoanalysis: the detective, like the analyst, seeks some evil in the past to be identified, faced, and controlled or defeated. Only then can the symbolic, never-ending struggle begin again.

Jung, at one time a disciple of Freud's, who split with him on a variety of issues, in contrast assumes a shared experience. Whereas Freud is most at home in dealing with illness or problem, Jung is most at home trying to explain the human experiences we all have, whether traumatic or not. A simple, but by no means meaningless, statement might be that Freud deals most strongly with explaining the psychological state of mental illness or problem and Jung deals with explaining the psychological state of what we assume to be mental health.

Erikson, drawing heavily from Freud and some from Jung, has been interested in exploring those recurrent patterns we all supposedly share in our lives. If a Jungian analysis can propose that horror and science fiction are cultural presentations of the struggle we all face in developing from birth to death and possibly beyond, an Erikson approach focuses upon the social aspects of comedy and the pain of going through the social life cycles of individualism, romance, marriage, family, and institutions.

All three approaches demonstrate that the supposedly transparent act of entertainment in such formulas as detective stories, horror and science fiction, and comedy are in fact very meaningful acts for those who watch the individual forms and are moved by them.

A word of caution is needed. Applying a particular approach—Freud to detective tales, for example—is not an indication that this is the only approach, the right approach, or even the best approach. We could just as well have applied Jung to the detective tale or the work of Alfred Adler to the news. What counts, perhaps, is the demonstration of the application. The reader can judge which, if any, approach he or she finds most valuable or wishes to pursue.

This section is intended to introduce the reader to a range of psychological models and some ways in which they can inform our study of television. The reader who finds this a helpful approach will want to explore more fully these or other psychological models and experiment with his or her own applications.

—9—
A Jungian Approach to Science Fiction and Horror

In discussing horror, the temptation is strong to talk in terms of affect, to let whether a particular media presentation scares us or not be a required part of the definition of horror. The problem with such an approach to definition is that, since people are frightened by different things, we can never have a common definition of the genre. This lack of agreement about what precisely is horrifying or disturbing makes affect a problematic approach for criticism. The same problem emerges when we attempt to define comedy on the basis of whether it makes us laugh. It is probably more fruitful for the critic to define the genre in terms of the elements we might expect it to comprise rather than by the reaction it elicits from the audience.

Until recently, horror was most frequently set in the past or in settings that evoked the past: gothic castles, exotic places, old cellars and attics. These settings are so firmly fixed that comic variations like "The Munsters" and "The Addams Family" were able to lampoon the horror genre by evoking the appropriate setting. But in the last decade, particularly on television, a new setting for horror shows has developed. The traditional exotic settings have given way to everyday urban and institutional settings. "The Night Stalker," to which we will return, is a good example of a combination of the old-style horror tale with contemporary locations.

Science fiction, on the other hand, has most often been based upon a projection into a potentially frightening future. "Star Trek" will serve as a primary example of the genre.

Beyond setting, however, one could consider character types, as does Karen Blair in her book *Meaning in Star Trek*. Other approaches include looking at patterns of narrative or at specific themes. For example, some critics have related science fiction to fear of the future and to concern about the meaning and possible dangers of progress. Against this concern, there has been a kind of faith in the future in spite of the dangers involved.

In science fiction, these two paradoxical attitudes, that we are our own worst enemy and that the future holds promise, are generally reconciled, particularly in television science fiction. Whereas horror has been presented as a dark milieu, a genre of night and nightmare, science fiction has tended toward the light: the dangers and trials not of dreams but of what might soon be our waking technology.

Before turning to "Star Trek" as an example, we need a brief explanation of the Jungian approach that will be used in the analysis. We are drawing on but a portion of a larger body of Jung's theory and applying it to a particular genre.

Self and Ego

A crucial beginning is Jung's use of the concepts of Self and of Ego to indicate two quite different ideas. Jung uses Self to relate how the individual sees himself or herself as a part of a larger social, mythic, or religious entity. The Self is an expression of one's relationship to some totality, such as the family, tribe, religious community, or nation. Identification with Self is an acknowledgment that a group identity is more important than the "I." The Ego, on the other hand, is the expression of one's uniqueness and separateness from any community identity. Jung and others have suggested that we are born in a state of Selfness: we have no Ego. That is, in this initial mode of Selfness, we have no understanding of what we are as individuals. We do not know that we *are* individuals; we are simply part of something larger, and, furthermore, there is no understanding of what that is. Since there is no sense of "I," there is no initial fear of the loss of Ego, no fear of death, for example, for there is no "I" to be concerned about.

A very important part of the Self-image, for any individual, is the symbol of the circle. The circle, or mandala, is a universal sign of wholeness and symmetry. The circle, like the Self and unlike the Ego, has no beginning and no end. Support for this idea can be found in the work of Rhoda Kellogg in San Francisco. Kellogg ran a center for children in which she encouraged them to draw whatever they wanted. Kellogg collected more than a million drawings by children, some of which appear in *Man and His Symbols,* edited by Jung shortly before he died. In her studies, Kellogg found that, when children first draw with a representational coherence that adults can recognize, they draw people as circles. A person appears as a circle with arms and legs. It confuses the child if you ask where the body is. To the child, the circle with arms and legs is a perfectly reasonable symbol of the wholeness of the person. Only as the child develops an Ego picture that is separate from the Self will he or she begin to draw a head with a trunk, to make a picture of one person different from that of another person.

The Ego and the Self are value-free concepts in Jungian analysis. One may develop either a positive or negative Ego and Self. When we deal with science fiction or horror, often the Self-image will turn out to be a negative one. At other times, it will be positive. Sometimes, the developing Ego will be positive; and other times, negative. Jung said the reason for this is that the whole process of Ego-Self separation is an ongoing, never-ending tension. The individual sees himself or herself as a separate entity and yet needs to relate to a Self-image. Each individual faces the constant problem of coming to some sort of rapport between Ego and Self. The Ego and the Self are symbolic of tendencies with the human personality. Jung did not use them as literal entities, but as metaphors for a process. One starts without any separate identity and then begins developing an Ego identity. There is always the danger that the individual will move entirely into one or the other mode of identity. Too much reliance upon Self leads to an identity entirely connected to the group and suggests a loss of will, while an excess of Ego can produce an entirely antisocial person.

As Rhoda Kellogg discovered with children's drawings, the circle is a dominant symbol of the Self. Karen Blair points out in *Meaning in Star Trek* that such Self-images are very clear in "Star Trek." The view of the top of the starship *Enterprise* itself and its orbit around a particular planet represent the affirmative Self-image of the spaceship community. The alien planet forms a second circle indicative of an alternate Self-image. Two communities exist with which one might potentially identify. A reading of Jung suggests that there are many potential Self-images that the individual can adopt—for example, parental images, religious or cult images, the political party, an organization or institution. Individuals and their mythologies often strive to achieve a balance between Ego and Self and among the multitude of potential Self-images.

Persona, Shadow, Anima, and Animus

Three primary figures that affect the development of a balanced Self-image are the *Persona,* the *Shadow,* and the *Anima* or *Animus.* The *Persona* represents the role a person takes on or develops to display his or her conscious understanding. The *Shadow* is a figure of the same sex who represents that which an individual attempts to deny although it is undeniably part of him. Jung taught that all people have within themselves traits connected with ideas of maleness and femaleness. For the male, the *Anima* figure represents those personality traits within himself that he identifies with the female. The *Animus* is the male figure who serves the same purpose for women.

The Persona is the image of the individual that others see and to which the individual is wedded. One's Persona is generally created by the culture, which casts the individual in a role, and the individual, who accepts that role. When the Anima/Animus or the Shadow exerts itself, the individual may feel uneasy with his or her Persona, may feel that it is simply a mask, perhaps even an iron mask that is almost impossible to tear away. In "Star Trek," Captain Kirk must maintain his Persona of the balanced leader, the mediator between emotionalism and logic. However, in many "Star Trek" episodes, Kirk's Shadow vies for expression. For example, in one episode ("The Enemy Within"), Kirk becomes two people: a ruthless, aggressive coward and a meek and somewhat indecisive pacifist. When this takes place, the crew's image of the Kirk Persona is shaken. They are reluctant to accept or recognize the possibility that the mask of Kirk is not the real Kirk. The liberated and dangerous Kirk then strives to convince the crew that the new Kirk is the proper, undeniable Persona; and Kirk, indeed, ends by embracing his dark side. In both this episode in which Kirk is split into two personalities and another ("Mirror, Mirror"), in which an evil Kirk from an alternate world and the Kirk of the *Enterprise* switch places, there is a tension created followed by a movement toward reestablishing Kirk's former Persona.

The Persona as mask is perhaps best exemplified in the final "Star Trek" episode ("Turnabout Intruder"), in which Kirk's mind is transferred into a woman's body. The transmuted Kirk is accepted as Anima and not as Kirk, although he gives evidence of his identity. In all these examples, the implication is that Kirk, or anyone else, has within him a shadow and an Anima or Animus, either of which can assert itself and alter the Persona. The assertion can be a terrible experience for Kirk or for us, but it can be one that helps in the process of individuation. This is made clear in the episode of the split Kirk, in which the meek Kirk realizes that he must join with the evil Kirk if his Persona is to be reestablished, but, at the same time, the Persona Kirk learns that the Shadow Kirk is an important part of his whole personality. The Shadow side is evil, but Captain Kirk comes to recognize that he needs the dark side of himself. It contains aspects of the captain that are necessary to his and the ship's survival.

The third impulse that any individual has is that of the Anima or Animus. While the Shadow is always of the same sex as the individual, the Anima or Animus represents the impulses of the opposite sex. A male has an Anima; and a female, an Animus. In developing a sense of sexual identity as a man or a woman, one comes to identify certain characteristics as typically male and others as typically female. Whether one attributes this to biology, myth, or culture, each individual has this experience as he or she develops. Thus, as the child experiences gender identification, he or she will see some responses as appropriate and others as alien. This creates a problem as to what to do with those alien aspects each individual finds within himself or herself. Jung suggests that the sexual other in each of us can be projected outward onto an Anima or Animus figure. However, to be a whole as an individuated person, the male must also accept his Anima and the female, her Animus. In Western culture, a male's Anima often represents the impulse away from logic, moving toward emotions and mystery. For a woman, the Animus figure is usually an impulse *toward* logic, control, and physical assertion.

As people develop, these metaphors of Persona, Shadow, and Anima/Animus are acting on their lives. The Persona suggests one way of being; the Shadow, another; and the Anima/Animus, a third. The interplay of the three determines what is appropriate and what is negative behavior. The Persona, Anima/Animus, and Shadow represent the desires to conform and to be different; and they each play a part in the individual's Ego development.

Mother, Daughter, Amazon, and Medium

Jung posited *types* that function as models for Anima, Persona, and Shadow, and he divided them by sex. Listed as female are the types known as Mother, Daughter, Amazon, and Medium. The Mother and the Medium are impulses toward the static and the Self, or collective identity. The Daughter and the Amazon figures are impulses toward dynamic individual Ego development.

In the media, these types are usually related to a female protagonist; it is difficult to discuss them in relation to "Star Trek" because the hero in that show is almost always male. The female types could easily be explored within the soap opera or in examples of science fiction that have female protagonists—for example, *Alien, Terror Train,* and *Halloween I* and *II*.

According to Jung, the Mother represents the female collective orientation to people. In American popular mythology, the projected Mother represents the protective homemaking and sheltering attitude. In a male-oriented tale, the woman who functions primarily as a Mother tends to see the man in terms of his social collective function as Father and protector of the family rather than as an individual. If there is a Mother figure, the Mother tends to direct the individuating figure toward a proper Persona, a proper relationship to the world. Over and over again in television, when you see someone identified as a Mother, the person will tend to impel the male protagonist toward how she should behave as a proper social figure, how he should look to other people: how he should dress, how he should talk, and what his ambitions should be in terms of his family and his job. This collective orientation does not have to be an affirmative one. There can be negative Mothers who support a negative status quo. In film, there are many examples, such as *Bloody Mama* and *Big Bad Mama*, gangster tales in which the Mother keeps the family together by doing things that are not socially acceptable. This rarely happens on television. There the Mother will tend to be a powerful affirmation of the culture's image of what is proper.

The Daughter directs attention to the Shadow. The figure needn't literally be a Daughter; what Jung tried to do was indicate a primal family and the metaphorical images a primal family tends to take on. The Daughter is a seductress, nymph, or possibly a beautiful witch or harlot. Unlike the Mother, she encourages acting out of self-interest and staying away from concrete commitment. She encourages movement toward the Shadow.

If one gives in totally to the Mother, one doesn't develop an Ego. If one gives in totally to the daughter, one becomes as one with the Shadow, which usually leads to destruction. It is particularly clear in horror that the seductive female who appears is really a monster and that the hero has to control himself and not give in emotionally to that Anima figure, that female impulse toward one's feelings, which will lead to his destruction.

The Amazon has the impulse toward the dynamic, toward change. The Amazon is presented as an independent comrade/competitor rather than a wife or potential lover. Here again, it can be a positive or negative image. In positive form, an Amazon such as Wonder Woman is an impulse toward independence. In negative form, such as the Cat Woman in "Batman," the Amazon is an impulse toward uncontrolled aggression. Since she cannot be obeyed like the Mother nor married like the Daughter, this competitive woman is presented as a powerful encouragement to Ego development and social isolation.

The last-mentioned female figure, the Medium, has a mystical connotation. She is not necessarily a mystic, but the metaphor is almost always mystical. In a positive presentation, the Medium might take the form of a seer or fortune teller, a person who can see into the future.

Father, Son, Hero and Wise Man

Paralleling and balancing the female figures in a Jungian system are those of the male, including Father, Son, Hero, and Wise Man. The Father has tended to correspond in one way to the Mother: they both represent the collective form of the personal function, the Self. They represent structure, order, and collective authority, whether they are respected or ridiculed. They are lords, kings, protectors, or, in more contemporary tales, bosses.

One of the difficulties the Father figure must face, particularly in science fiction such as "Star Trek," is that he does not know his children (his subjects) as individuals. The children frequently cry out to be recognized as individuals and not projections of what the Father wants them to be. In "Star Trek," the leader of a planet, whether a good leader or a bad one, often must learn from Captain Kirk and the *Enterprise* crew that, even though he has the responsibility for his people as a group, he also has to regard them as individuals. The Fathers tend, in all forms, toward the tragic. They arouse in others the will to power which the Father represents. He represents keeping things the way they are, with the Father in charge. He demands giving oneself up to Self, not having any individuality, not even recognizing any Ego development, because that could threaten the whole structure.

The Son (or Brother) figure threatens the structure. This is presented as a natural process. He is in rebellion and expresses individualism and personal concerns. Metaphorically, what is almost always the object of rebellion on television in general, and in science fiction in particular, is what the Father represents, the impulse toward the collective. The Sons are usually loners. They are not concerned with permanent relations with other people, because the Father represents just that. The Sons can be companions or enemies; but, since they threaten what the Father stands for, they are dangerous figures.

The Hero tends to be dynamic and outgoing. Masculine, oriented toward objective, collective values, the Hero greatly affirms the Father. He is not a loner or a rebel; he is the soldier, the go-getter who fights, strives, and accomplishes for the collective. That is the general frame of reference in which heroism is portrayed: not as rebellion but as a force for good within an affirmative collective. Villains, then, are those who threaten the collective. Ultimately, the Hero is affirming social values, fighting against those things which threaten the collective and/or the image of the Father.

Although it is neither a horror series nor a science fiction series, "Happy Days" presents a clear example of a character moving from one type to another. Fonzie's character originally represented the Son, someone in conflict with society. He had not done what was conformist and acceptable and was a trial to the severely conformist adults. As Fonzie became a popular focus for the narrative, he gradually became more of a conformist figure. He changed from being a Son to being a Hero, affirming the Father. The importance of the Father, in television Westerns particularly, is rather striking. Even if the Father does wrong, failing to recognize his children as individuals, ultimately what he is doing is protected as right.

It is important that the Hero be neither receptive nor wise. He has to sense the right thing to do. He has to feel it. Heroism does not require desire for change. In fact, it requires just the opposite: loyalty and a conviction that the way of the collective, of the Self, is the proper way.

Another masculine type, the Wise Man, is idea oriented rather than person oriented. The Wise Man does not necessarily counsel toward a particular kind of behavior. He does not fight like the Hero, but listens, receives, and perceives. When we encounter a Wise Man, he is frequently a teacher, scholar, sage, or philosopher. Usually an older figure, he is not interested in power or necessarily in people. Our traditional picture of the Wise Man is the hermit, who does not want to have anything to do with people, with either Self-image or Ego.

"The Incredible Hulk" in Light of Jung

One difficulty we have in popular culture, and specifically in television, is the desire to incorporate Wise Man figures into the total collective affirmative position. When we encounter a Wise Man, frequently from a different culture from that of the protagonist, he is forced to support the affirmative Father. This recurs in "The Incredible Hulk," particularly those episodes that involve the elderly Japanese man who runs a school for meditation and related martial arts. He himself is blind; yet he is presented as having a great sense of perception about what is going on around him, and he is very wise and all-knowing. He triumphed in all three episodes in which he appeared. Initially, he was presented as a Wise Man; but he very soon became a Father, particularly in the third episode in which he died. At the beginning of that episode, he told us that he was going to die because his own Self-knowledge was a part of what separated him from this culture. In *Star Wars,* the same thing happened. Obi Wan Kenobi knew he was going to die, and he was a Wise Man. He did not want to take on the image of the Father. Instead, he counseled Luke toward individuation, not toward accepting him as a Father. Luke could not hang onto him; Obi did not want that, nor did he want Luke ultimately to rebel against him. A protagonist's desire to see a Wise Man as a potential Father is a repeated problem. Again and again, the Wise Man must say: "Go and don't cling to me; be yourself; move toward individuation."

"The Incredible Hulk" is an interesting examination of this kind of interaction. David Banner constantly says figuratively and almost literally, "My Shadow keeps erasing my Persona." In the course of the series, however, the Hulk himself, like the Fonz, ultimately has become a hero. He started off in the first episode as a totally uncontrollable animal, a Shadow perceived as evil. As the series progressed, however, he gradually became a pussycat. He never hurt anybody seriously, not even villains. He became a protector of the weak. The Shadow figure was totally incorporated and was no longer negative for the viewer. Although David Banner still went around saying, "I want to be free of this horrible thing," it had, for the audience, ceased to *be* a horrible thing: it had become an embarrassing creature related to the fear of being revealed for what one is, fear of being naked in the street, fear of the loss of control, primal fear. So over and over again, David Banner seeks Wise Men or Anima, women he cannot hold on to. Two of them have gotten killed, and he ultimately has had to leave all of them. He is constantly looking for someone to tell him how to control his Shadow rather than to accept it.

"Star Trek" in Light of Jung

To apply these Jungian ideas, we can now examine one "Star Trek" episode, "Assignment Earth," in which Captain Kirk confronts a character named Gary Seven, played in the episode by Robert Lansing. Gary Seven has been trained by an advanced civilization on a distant planet to come to earth to keep humanity from destroying itself. Seven is accidentally beamed aboard the *Enterprise* while Kirk is accidentally visiting the twentieth-century United States. Kirk, however, cannot decide whether to believe or disbelieve Seven. Since Seven is on a deadline to stop a missile launching, Kirk has to make up his mind quickly, especially when Seven escapes. Kirk and Spock trail the elusive Gary Seven, who travels with a mysterious cat to whom he speaks, and finally trap him in front of a secret computer Seven plans to use to stop the missile flight. Since Seven is the only one who can handle the computer, Kirk has to make a quick decision about whether to trust him. When Seven performs an unselfish act, Kirk decides to rely on Seven's word that he is out to save humanity from itself. Kirk proves to be right, and the episode ends with Seven remaining on earth in the twentieth century to help humanity, while Kirk and Spock return to the *Enterprise* to move forward into the future.

Captain Kirk is responsible for exploring new worlds, but he also makes it clear several times in the episode that he has a responsibility for not changing future or past history. His meeting with Gary Seven requires that he struggle with that responsibility. What are the ethical implications of acting or not acting? Gary Seven says that he is a projection of perfect Self-image, and he behaves that way. He has been trained for generations; yet, he seems to have little or no ego interest at all. He has been sent to earth simply to save others, and he has total dedication to the task. Kirk, however, does not know that. Kirk, who cannot assess Seven's placid, untroubled Persona, perceives him as a

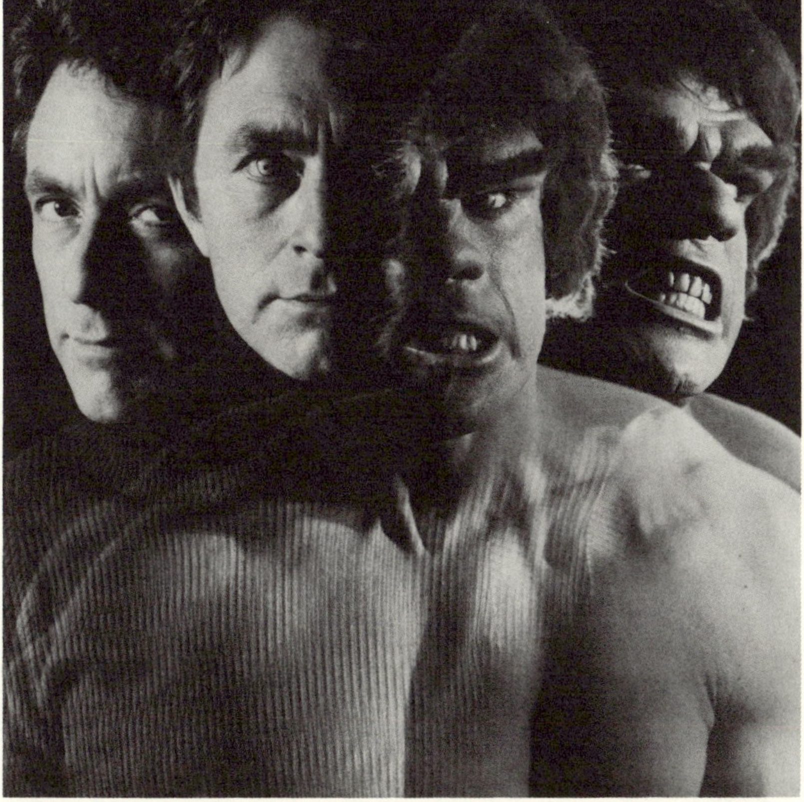

Bill Bixby in "The Incredible Hulk."

Shadow or as a potential Shadow and then proceeds accordingly. Kirk's ultimate difficulty in dealing with Gary Seven is resolved in the confrontation at the computer in which Kirk has to make up his mind how he views Gary Seven. That problem is resolved when Gary Seven engages in an action Kirk accepts as morally correct.

Over and over again, the life of the *Enterprise* revolves around Kirk and how he sees his identity as the captain. It is a Persona problem in which Kirk is often impelled by responsibility to see himself as a Gary Seven, a person with no Ego. Therefore, the show very frequently emphasizes that Kirk has feelings and impulses and that these emotions are what make him different from Spock and what make most of his decisions painful ones, paralleling those we face constantly. Kirk is almost always presented as the character in the process of individuation. It is a tough, fluctuating position for Kirk, since he must *behave* as a Father.

It is fairly obvious what Spock represents. He is a Wise Man, always counseling rationality and logic. Spock supposedly has no emotions (except, as Karen Blair points out, once every so many years, when a mating instinct takes over).

In the "Assignment Earth" episode, Gary Seven, a strong Hero figure, is paired with a cat. The cat is an ancient Anima figure that propels Seven toward Ego. The two are presented as one until we find that the cat takes the form of a woman. Her erratic behavior and jealousy seem to balance his Selfness and thus to humanize his strongly dehumanized Persona.

In contrast to Spock in the series and Gary Seven in the episode discussed, we have Doctor McCoy. Although he is a scientist, McCoy is tempered by emotionalism and counsels Kirk toward emotionalism. We have a balance around Kirk; total logic in the person of Spock and, on the other side, McCoy and his call to emotion. McCoy wants to act, to save people without worry about the consequences. According to McCoy, if someone is a part of the *Enterprise,* he deserves help. Don't listen to Spock, the Wise Man; follow your Anima, and take chances.

Although he is not ultimately the person of action, we have the counsel of a potential Hero in McCoy; but both Spock and McCoy can only counsel. The action must be taken by Kirk. Spock can say, "We must behave logically"; but it is Kirk who has to decide whether or not he *is* going to behave logically. McCoy can say, "You must act"; but McCoy doesn't act. Ultimately, the actor must be Kirk. He's the one who has to face the monster. Even McCoy, who counsels for individualism, does not rebel against Kirk and the whole.

"Kolchak: The Night Stalker" in Light of Jung

Because there are currently few science-fiction or horror series on television, it is difficult to suggest contemporary series to complement the "Star Trek" example and that of "The Incredible Hulk," with the notable exception of England's "Dr. Who," which has been a weekly series on British TV since 1962. The show, like "The Night Stalker," which is still on in reruns, can be used as a focus to further demonstrate these ideas.

"The Night Stalker" hero was, at first glance, the most unlikely heir to Dracula's pursuer, Dr. Van Helsing, that one could imagine. Carl Kolchak wore a rumpled lightweight seersucker summer suit, often out of season, a distinctive and not particularly attractive straw hat, a tape recorder over one shoulder, and a camera over the other.

Kolchak, as the character evolved on the ABC Television series (based upon two highly successful made-for-television movies, *The Night Stalker,* 1972, and *The Night Strangler,* 1973), was very much a man of the media. He was apparently a paranoid Hero, but his paranoia always turned out to be based on reality—although even the reality of his monsters may be questionable, since each tale in the series was narrated by Kolchak, who might not have been a totally reliable narrator.

Generally, "Kolchak: The Night Stalker" opened with a ghastly murder narrated by Kolchak. He told us that some horror had been let loose on an unsuspecting public, and it was made clear to us that Kolchak had somehow survived this horror and was about to tell us the tale. Invariably, Kolchak told his story to a tape recorder, preserving a diary for future posterity and Self, very much like Jonathan Harker (in Bram Stoker's *Dracula),* for no one in Kolchak's world was willing to believe or listen to him. Though he told the truth, he had to face the pain of never being believed. In the episode "The Werewolf," for example, Kolchak told his tape recorder of his encounter with a werewolf aboard a ship. Behind Kolchak, a dock porter patiently waited, paying no attention to the eccentric man talking to his machine and spewing out his nightmare from start to finish. Often Kolchak recorded at his own desk in the office of International News Service, where his fellow workers, like the dock porter, ignored him completely. It was Kolchak's nightmare, not theirs. The world would not listen, as it would not listen to the warnings of Dr. Miles Binnell in Don Siegel's film *Invasion of the Body Snatchers* or of David Vincent in the television series "The Invaders." Binnell, Vincent, and Kolchak brought a warning of the possibility of the end of the world and were considered madmen or frauds for doing so.

In the "Kolchak" series, following the initial crime, the titles for the show came on. One credit was placed over a scene of Kolchak alone at his desk, typing. He heard something. He turned. Freeze frame close-up of Kolchak, frightened, but at his machine. His was a world of paranoia realized.

In addition to the tape recorder Kolchak utilized to talk to himself and retain his sanity, he had two other tools, the typewriter and the camera. The evidence of the camera, the pictures he took of monsters, were invariably destroyed or not believed. The hard evidence of the photo was of no value to Kolchak. His other professional tool, the typewriter, was equally ignored. Thus, neither word nor image was accepted as evidence.

The series was set in Chicago, a rather strange Chicago in keeping with the horror show. In fact, Chicago is equated with quite a different violent genre, the gangster tale. Several times in the series, Kolchak did become involved with gangsters, resulting in a rather strange mix. In "The Zombie," a series of gangland murders was being committed by a zombie. In "The Spanish Moss Murders," Kolchak's boss, Tony (Simon Oakland), tried to get Carl to cover a gangland murder, but the genre clearly didn't interest the erratic reporter. "They're all the same," bleated Kolchak. "Nobody talks. Nobody says anything. Routine."

Kolchak's desire was to make the public aware of nightmare and shadow, not social corruption and violence. Kolchak's goal was a kind of public shock psychoanalysis. Let the public know the truth about the horror it nurtures: the vampires equated with fear of disease, the werewolves equated with our fear of losing self-control, the zombies equated with the fear of losing our will. A recurrent motif in the series was Kolchak's discovery that the monster indeed had been created from the human psyche; for example, a monster from the bayou country had been released by the repressed nightmare of a man undergoing sleep research in "The Spanish Moss Murders." The parallel, perhaps, can be seen with the monster from the id in the movie *Forbidden Planet,* a monster patterned overtly on Caliban, the repressed monster of Shakespeare's *The Tempest*. In any case, Kolchak generally found himself to be a kind of unheeded amateur public psychologist.

Yet, each time Kolchak tried to get his story on the wires of INS, he was stopped, forced away from the public forum to the private diary, the tape recorder. The public, like the troubled dreamer, did not want to face the meaning of the dream when the analyst forced its truth into the open. Adding to Kolchak's frustration was a vast institutional rejection of his inquiry. Not only did the public, but the government and the professions rejected Kolchak's warnings. Police lieutenants, ship captains, hospital administrators, and all other representatives of established order shouted at him, abused him, and tried to keep him and themselves from the truth. Inevitably, the police or an authority figure was forced by events and the reporter to face the horror he could not understand. Once this horror had been faced and defeated, however, the representative, the parental figure, refused to challenge the social view of the order of things and acknowledge that terrors existed beyond the power of his profession to handle. The police denied Kolchak, his boss refused to print his story, and he was forced to turn to his tape recorder and speak to himself. In fact, it sometimes happened that the shows ended with Kolchak suffering the traditional messianic fate: not only was he denied after providing the key to salvation, but he was also imprisoned or cast out. It was common for Kolchak to be accused of the murder of a human being, since society could not accept that he had not destroyed a *human* but a monster threatening humankind. Kolchak's fate for saving humanity was to be called a madman, a murderer, or a fool.

Generally, Kolchak sought an outside ally, someone with special powers, someone representing religion or mysticism, a contact with a forgotten Self or an Anima that could lead to salvation. Kolchak's allies, like those of many other messianic figures, were the social outcasts: witch doctors, gypsies, religious mystics. Generally, too, his acquired allies would abandon him or die when the moment of final confrontation came. In "The Energy Eater," a Native American witch doctor, played by William Smith, ran away from a hospital upon being threatened by an Indian spirit; in "Horror in the Heights," an eighty-year-old East Indian, played by Abraham Sofaer, was too feeble to destroy the monster. Kolchak, denied by friends, boss, society, and allies, would be forced to take on the horror himself, to stand alone and face the dark image of the human psyche, and to have no satisfaction beyond symbolic altruism.

Each monster encountered had the potential to destroy the world (or at least Chicago); and Kolchak, the rumpled, wisecracking, middle-aged reporter with the nonheroic name would become the hero, would face and destroy that monster. Kolchak was not a spiritual figure or a scientist, common as the savior in the genre; he was a reporter, a representative of the nonmystical and the nonscientific. He was in many ways a common man.

It was always Kolchak who had to step forward with the ancient tools and face the evil directly. Simple guns were always useless. Kolchak, armed with a stake, the sharpened branch of a swamp tree, a crossbow, silver bullets, the needle and thread to sew up the mouth of a zombie, had to stand face to face with the creature. Occasionally, Kolchak may have run screaming; but he always recovered and turned and faced the evil and the unknown—he always faced the nightmare.

As stated earlier, the Chicago of "Kolchak: The Night Stalker" was a netherworld in the middle of the United States—an unreal city. We frequently saw Kolchak driving down State Street past the Chicago Theater, down the Outer Drive, past the Hancock Building. We saw the icons of a Chicago that the world could supposedly recognize. We had roots in a supposedly real city. Yet, when we got into each episode, we had a dreamlike city more like Kafka's or Brecht's image of the United States than the "real" thing. We had a place called Roosevelt Heights, which looked like a lower-middle-class, urban Jewish neighborhood of the 1940s. No such place exists. We had a place, supposedly on the South Side, where Southern fiddlers played happily on street corners for quarters. No such place exists. What we had in the show was a series of idealized neighborhoods of our urban past, followed by generalized attacks on those memories by horrible creatures.

The monsters Kolchak encountered were extensions of the American horror monsters we know. Yet, they were often more brutal—killing dozens, defiling the bodies—and more importantly, less secretive. From the first vampire in Las Vegas to the werewolf on board a ship, the monsters in "Kolchak: The Night Stalker" did not need to hide, to lurk. They were like urban crime in the streets; yet society did not wish to recognize the fact. Only Kolchak, religious mystics, and the very old were willing to acknowledge the streetwalking horror; and only Kolchak, the ne'er-do-well next door, was willing to face it. Kolchak's role as reporter, conscience of the public, gradually threatened evil; and he became a potential victim.

Kolchak's world was an enclosed one. We never saw him as a human outside of his job. He had no friends other than contacts and colleagues. He appeared to have no interests other than his job. His co-workers, like the police and the socially acceptable, were a hindrance rather than a help; yet they were his only family. His boss, a bumbling Father figure, never believed his stories. Ron (Jack Grinnage), his fellow worker, was a complete pragmatist, a smug brother, a young man with facts about everything at his fingertips, in contrast to Carl, the man of vision. Ron never left the office; Carl was restless in it. The other primary co-worker was Emily (Ruth McDevitt). Emily was the Mother. She constantly championed senior citizens and resented comments about the enfeebled, the ancient. She was forever asserting her rights and going on dates. This life affirmation, the very thing Kolchak tried to champion, made her Kolchak's best friend. In "Horror in the Heights," Kolchak was told that the monster took on the appearance of the person the victim most trusts. Kolchak announced with confidence that he trusted no one. The monster appeared to him as Emily, and Kolchak had to fire a crossbow directly at her image. The traumatic murder was accepted by Kolchak without blinking.

Thus, the problem Kolchak faced inside his office was familial, represented by the rational, unfeeling young Ron on the one hand and the life-affirming, emotional, older Emily on the other. Between them stood the vacillating Tony, who had to act as judge and who always voted for the brother. Kolchak was the errant son.

Outside of the familial office scene, Kolchak also stood between two forces opposed to his inquiry—the officials of society (Self), on the one hand, who operated in daytime and were, like Ron, rationalists; and the horror creatures of the night (Shadow), the irrational, emotional, physical monsters. Caught between was the populace, which was decimated, and Kolchak, their unrecognized hero, who avenged them without reward and accepted the lonely burden of defying both the rational and irrational. Kolchak, perhaps like most viewers, lived in a state of nervous balance between Ego and Self. Solutions were a matter, not of choosing sides, but of facing the terror of life alone.

Kolchak himself was a life-affirming creature of great vitality. He was constantly in motion, compulsively talking, joking, probing, and making himself vulnerable. At the same time, his job made him an outsider, an intruder with whom most people in authority did not wish to deal. Kolchak had to force himself on them. Kolchak was the outcast here, unappreciated by his colleagues, society, and the public. Publicly, he was a clown and a nuisance. In press conferences, which were depicted frequently in the series, he asked embarrassing questions, separating himself from his fellow reporters. His public face was seen in the light of day, and he was treated without respect by a series of smug officials played by such character actors as Keenan Wynn, John Dehner, William Daniels, and Severn Darden. An ultimate irony of Kolchak was that he engaged in a public profession, yet his satisfactions were never public.

Finally, the monsters of the series were traditional in that they represented an immortal evil; yet none of them felt the remorse we have so often come to expect in horror in the media. In that sense, the series did not come to terms with morality as have so many American horror films in the past. We had no anguished monsters, no creatures crying for release in random rational moments. The horror of "Kolchak: The Night Stalker" was the horror of the street, the horror of violence, the horror of a darkly dreamlike urban setting. Our hero was not the traditional savior of horror films who can bring us to terms with mortality through religion or scientific knowledge. Our hero was a not terribly bright reporter who accepted that horror exists, that it is violent and sudden, and that it was his (and possibly our) responsibility to face it.

In fact, humor in the series was often derived from an understanding that Kolchak was indeed a strange savior, perhaps an unworthy man elevated by chance, fear, and professional zeal to protect society. He was not unique in this. Reporters as probers and representatives of society have appeared in many horror films as heroes (*The Mysterious Dr. X* and *Murders in the Wax Museum,* for example) or clowns (*Mad Love; The Mysterious Mr. Wong).* In the past, however, the reporter has fallen back on the police, a religious figure, or a scholar to help him defeat evil. In "Kolchak: The Night Stalker," as we have seen, Kolchak was rejected by all; and, in the end, he was a man alone—alone with the monster, alone with his tale, rumpled, frightened, nervously amused, perhaps unreliable, but ever vigilant in a frightening fantasy of contemporary urban terror.

Summary

The Jungian model proposed in this chapter provides a means of looking at the narrative milieu of "Star Trek," "The Night Stalker," or "The Incredible Hulk" as a series of problems of individuation. Each episode presents a challenge to the individual or collective Ego/Self axis. Each episode provides a different series of antagonisms and challenges to the process of individuation. A monster is not simply a monster. It becomes a fragment threatening the conservative health of the society. As Kolchak, David Banner, and the *Enterprise* "boldly go where no man has gone before," they bring with them a solid commitment to Self (Star Command, civilization, the well-being of the inbred community) which withstands all attempts to cause the individual ego to rebel.

It is important to point out, however, that "Star Trek," "The Night Stalker," and "The Incredible Hulk" are not unusual in this, nor are they uniquely open to Jungian analysis. Jungian psychology provides a narrative model which can aid in the exploration of a wide variety of popular material.

—10—
Erik Erikson's Life Cycles as Related to Comedy

Early in *Regeneration through Violence,* Richard Slotkin writes:

> Mythology is a complex of narratives that dramatizes the world vision and historical sense of a people or culture, reducing centuries of experience into a constellation of compelling metaphors.

Cultural experience is reduced in one sense. But "reduced" is not used pejoratively; it means shaped to a meaning. History is reduced to a set of metaphors so that it can be understood. One way of examining a generic form is to explore what those metaphors might be. Slotkin goes on to say:

> The ultimate source of myth is the human mind itself, for man is essentially a myth-making animal. He naturally seeks to understand his world in order to control it. And his first act encompassing this end is an act of the mind or imagination. On the basis of limited finite experience, he creates a hypothetical vision of a universal infinite order and imposes that hypothesis on his perception of the phenomenon of nature and his own behavior.

The myth isn't out there, according to Slotkin; the culture creates it. Individuals are involved as their tellings affect the shape of the mythic stories. Slotkin believes humans have a functional impulse to create myth. He suggests that we seek to find mythologies because we want to understand our world. The world is a complex, often confusing place that is not inherently reasonable. In making sense out of it, we must distort and reduce experiences so that it will be understandable.

If information does not have meaning, people create a meaning so that they can function on the basis of what they have experienced. We create a hypothetical vision. We present some tale of what our world might mean. That explanation might be about how families survive, how, in our culture, individuals make their way in society, or how one gets a job. We pose a hypothesis to explain the phenomena of nature and our own behavior. Again, simply put, we create these myths so that we can make sense out of the universe.

Often, we try to impose these myths upon our own behavior. We sometimes act as if things really are the way we have mythologized them; as Slotkin suggests, this creates a strange dynamic. Our experience does not work out the way "Cheers" works out. What we see in a television show is indeed a kind of myth, as opposed to a model for how we should behave; but it is almost impossible to remember that. Viewers face a complex question: Should we behave the way Diane and Sam behave? Is that a role model? If so, it is a problematic role model. Can we live that way?

Often, the term *situation comedy* is used to identify the comic presentation of these myths on television. However, the term *situation comedy* is problematic, for its meaning is unclear. It refers to a comedy about a situation, but all comedy grows out of some situation.

One way to proceed with a discussion of television comedy is to consider the protagonists' position in a life cycle. Drawing from life stages that Erik Erikson suggests, we can divide the comic cycle into four sections or focuses: individual, courtship, family, and institutional. In television, the last two are most evident. The forms are concurrent, and each one presents a different kind of mythology. We can look at where the protagonist exists in each form and how the form relates to the cycle. One begins as an individual, proceeds through some form of courtship, moves into a familial life, and then has to cope with an institutional situation—usually, but not always, a work situation. All comedy involves an aspect of conflict, and each of these comic forces has taken on particular kinds of conflicts. The tendency in individual comedy is for the individual to be in conflict with society. In courtship, the conflict is with a potential loved one and often represents a more general conflict between the sexes. Family comedies have often dealt with a conscious overresponsibility. Institutional comedies have tended to be about interpersonal relationships, how one gets along with other people. In each case, the individual is trying to get along and find a place in society.

Individual Comedy

In American comedy the central problem frequently stems from the infantile state of the individual protagonist. Still being an emotional and intellectual child, such a person can make no commitments, cannot become part of society. Television examples of such a character include the shows of Red Skelton, Tim Conway, Red Buttons, the Smothers Brothers, and Jerry Lewis. Jackie Gleason played such a character as a Ralph Kramden on "The Honeymooners." Ralph did succeed, but only by chance, intervention, or goodwill of somebody else, or his own painful decisions to accept maturity.

The wish of the protagonist to remain childish, to avoid joining society and entering the life cycle and thus to evade the adult issues of individuation, alienation, and death is often presented on television as comic. A good example is "The Honeymooners," which was presented as a lower-class potential tragedy. One of the things that kept the scenes comic was Ralph Kramden's unwillingness to accept an adult role. Kramden was an animalistic innocent like Chester Riley or George Jefferson. Almost all of the "Three's Company" episodes deal with these very issues.

Coupled with these innocents is a stable, parental partner. This provides a balance to the form. For instance, when Desi Arnaz left "I Love Lucy," a new parenting figure was found in Mr. Mooney. This parental partner always profits by the protagonist's infantile state. Because there is no assumption of equality, the parental partner may take advantage of the comic child-adult. The protagonist is caught between what it is to be a child, free to express oneself, and the responsibilities of adulthood. When one behaves like a baby, as funny and endearing as that might be, one cannot be accepted in society as an adult. It is a dilemma. The child is protected; the child is potentially magical; yet there are limitations beyond which a child may not go. The fruit of the tree of knowledge must be eaten.

There are two possible resolutions to an individual comedy: integration and acceptance into the society; or acceptance of separateness. In our society, comedies have tended toward integration and acceptance as an affirmative comic ending. But a strong pathetic tendency continues in our comedy, from Charlie Chaplin going down the road alone at the ending to alienated Woody Allen.

It is not socially more significant to have an acceptance of separateness; it is just closer to the possibility of tragedy. In our society, tragedy has always been accepted as more meaningful than comedy. There has always been an association between the kind of narrative and the meaning of the narrative. But comedies are not less meaningful than tragedies. In our lives, the tragic moments *may* be more meaningful; but it is a mistake to transfer that into a claim about the relative value of artistic works.

Individual comedy has not been a dominant form on television. This may, in part, reflect television's need for a larger audience than the single central figure is likely to attract. It may also reflect the relative lack of importance of the individual comic myth in the years since television became popular. For example, individual comedies were most popular in the films of the 1910s and 1920s. With the last big influx of immigration, the comic mode that dealt with the potential triumph of the individual was popular. At the end of the 1920s and into the 1930s, comedy teams or friendship groups became popular. By the time television emerged as a popular form, it is fairly clear that individual comic shows were in the minority.

In individual comedy, the very traditional idea, going back to Aristotle, of the intervention of fate is important. We have two factors operating in individual comedy. First, fate may intercede so that the person who could not triumph on his or her own succeeds. Second, one can succeed through the ability to improvise, to make do, a kind of aggressive go-getiveness. As in "Sergeant Bilko," it is almost a mechanical skill that does not relate to intelligence.

We could suggest another category called Friendship as a variation on the individual comedies. Friendship situations tend to be a way out of the problem of separateness. These tales are resolved in the end by bringing incomplete individuals together as a single organic whole. They all support each other. Laurel and Hardy had a tendency in their films not to be integrated or accepted. At the ending of one film, Hardy is killed and becomes a horse, and the final shot shows Laurel and the horse walking down the road together. At the end of another of their films, they have been turned into skeletons. That is the last we see of them. Television examples of such dependent friendships of incomplete partners include "Chico and the Man," "The Odd Couple," and "Laverne and Shirley."

Courtship Comedy

The primary problem in courtship comedies becomes the lack of experience with the other sex. Although this has increasingly come to mean literal sexual experience, the "experience" may be in coping with a courtship situation. In courtship comedy, the comic individual has moved into a relationship involving the other sex. Almost always, the male is presented as the one who has the lack of experience, the lack of courtship knowledge, because, in our mythology, the male has devoted himself thoroughly to work, to the pragmatic, while the female has devoted herself to emotions, interaction, and sexuality. Their encounter is presented as comic interaction of incompatibles who must adjust to each other if the species is to continue. "House Calls" presented such a dilemma.

Because of the episodic nature of series television, we seldom have a resolution to courtship comedy. If we do, we are moved into another category. What has tended to happen to the courtship comedy on television is a commitment, a move out of the courtship formula. Sometimes that movement has been very difficult. A good example of the difficulty was in the show "Rhoda." It started as a courtship comedy; then, after two seasons, Rhoda and Joe got married. This presented tremendous problems. The change in the situation required a whole new comic form. That which had been funny on "Rhoda" was no longer appropriate, which led to serious ratings problems. An attempt was made to return to individualism or courtship, but there is no turning back the life cycle.

Family Comedy

Family comedies tend to focus on the problem of being responsible for others. The families in television comedy tend to be patriarchal, so that the question to be treated comically is how the father will resolve some threat to the family's stability. There are some exceptions to this rule, such as "One Day at a Time" or Diahann Carroll's old show "Julia," but the clear majority of television families have centered around the father. From early in television's history with "Life of Riley," "Father Knows Best," and "Leave It to Beaver" to "Eight Is Enough," the primary comic character who is facing responsibility in the familial comedy has been the male head of the house. The point is not simply that most TV families have resident male heads but that the shows have presented the father as having responsibility for the family and focused comic attention upon his attempt to fulfill that responsibility. The male head of the family has the burden of dealing with society, the burden of making a living. He has difficulty in reconciling what he must do to make money with his personal commitments and ideals. What frequently happens is that the resolution takes the form of a confession in which the person says, "I really did do this." Archie Bunker confesses over and over again. He may be forced to confess reluctantly; but, for whatever reason, he *does* confess, and the situation returns to stasis. With each new episode, however, the threat to stability begins again. In the familial mythology, this never ends; each family must continually face the same problems. There are no solutions. The best it can do is move a little more toward some sort of stability—or at least the hope for stability. Almost every episode of a familial comedy involves comic presentation of potentially tragic threats to the stability of the family. Over the course of time, what is presented is process rather than resolution.

The confession of the family leader, usually the male parent, ushers in the return to stasis. He does something wrong because he feels he has to be responsible or does not want to look vulnerable; eventually he confesses, and everything works out all right, so that he is supported by his family and his self-image is confirmed. Tom Bradford on "Eight Is Enough" is an excellent example of such a figure. He continually makes a mistake, suffers, confesses, is affirmed by the family, and finally comes to some greater understanding of them.

Institutional Comedy

With institutional comedy, the problem of interpersonal relationships exposes our cultural complexity. A diverse group of people is thrown together, usually by their work. The "M*A*S*H" hospital is an example of this. How will they cope with the social group with which they must interact? The comic assumption is based on the inability of the individual to cope with the diversity of people he or she must get along with at the hospital.

There are a lot of similarities between the institutional and the familial series. Curiously, the one important thing that varies is that these people have less trouble getting along with each other than families do. In these situations, they must get along with each other to make a living. In one case we literally have a family; in the other case, we have people who have been put together and have to learn to get along with each other. One could start drawing parallels between family situations and some of the ongoing institutional shows. When we look at the "family" in an institutional show, the analogy breaks down in an interesting way. The family tends to be somewhat fragmented; someone is missing. There is no mother. There is a father figure; and, problematically, there are children. For instance, in "M*A*S*H" and "AfterMASH" obviously Colonel Potter functions as a paternal figure in relationship to other characters who make up a potential family.

Family and institutional presentations have tended, because of the evolution of culture, to be potentially important as metaphors for a very large portion of the audience. These are very serious aspects of one's life. On one level, we are talking about comedy; on another, about how people become part of their society.

It is very difficult to label a television comedy show and say, "It will always fit one form or another." There is usually a strong impulse toward one of the forms: individual, courtship, family, or institution, but there are also variations. We can look at a specific episode of a show, for example "Barney Miller," which is essentially an institutional show, and occasionally find one of the other forms.

"Mork and Mindy" is a good example of a show that moves between forms. Sometimes it functions as a courtship comedy; but, frequently, "Mork and Mindy" episodes run without Mork and Mindy presented in a courtship situation. Often, we have Mork alone, and the show moves into individual comedy. Mork is an alien trying desperately to fit into this society. He is presented as being infantile. The whole idea of the opening of "Mork and Mindy," when he comes from the egg, is that he is a newborn creature trying to understand his situation. Mork continues to act like a child. So, the individuation process goes on, over and over again, and he is never accepted. At the end of each episode, he is always separate, and he talks to Orson about how he still doesn't understand: something is wrong. At other times, episodes will involve the idea of courtship, or the show will focus on Mindy's relationship to her father and grandmother and move into the family formula.

In one sense, comedy is very closely akin to horror. It is interesting to compare what is presented as comedy and what is presented as horror. A kind of essence, particularly of American comedy, is the presentation of antagonism and threat to individual or group. The possibility of tragedy always hovers on the horizon of comedy. It is

David Groh and Valerie Harper in ''Rhoda.''

A special Thanksgiving episode of ''Archie Bunker's Place'' with, in back, Sally Struthers and Rob Reiner, and, in front, Carroll O'Connor, Dick Billingsley, Danielle Brisebois, and Jean Stapleton.

very rare to have something presented as comedy in which the comic basis of the incidents is not the potential for something horrible happening. Humor is based on the possibility of something happening which is not at all funny. At its most extreme or grossest level, the horrible event itself (and the fact that it does not result in tragedy) is presented as funny. In something like *The Three Stooges,* the very things that have the potential of tragedy appear literally to happen. They get nails pounded into their heads or fingers poked into their eyes, or they fall off buildings; but they do not die.

Comedy can affirm or challenge the audience's attitudes about the conflicts it explores. "The Mary Tyler Moore Show" tended to be very reinforcing, to say, "Don't feel guilty about the way you have thought about things; you are justified in feeling the way you do." You get the opposite in Norman Lear productions. Norman Lear productions repeatedly say, "Feel guilty about the way you think, the way you may have felt."

Different kinds of shows present different kinds of issues. It is very difficult to predict which format will be popular and which will not be popular. At different times, the audience will be drawn to different forms.

By applying Erikson's life stages in this way, we come to see why it is that different types of comedy take on different plot formulas. Each type lends itself to particular mythic questions, and our interest in these questions affects our interest in the show.

—11—

A Freudian Analysis of the Private Detective Tale

by Jeffrey H. Mahan

The development of psychoanalytic theory in this century has shaped the way most of us think about our experience. Even among those who profess to reject Freud and Freudianism, we find the concern for the unconscious, an awareness of the role of sexuality in human development, and a vocabulary (which many are surprised to find is psychoanalytic) including terms such as ego, Oedipus complex, and wish fulfillment.

Freud is certainly best known for his work on the human personality. His general ideas about the development of a healthy personality in which the *ego* balances the demands of the *id* and the *superego* are well established. It is less known that there is a rich Freudian social theory as well. Freud's interests were not limited to the individual personality but ranged widely, and his published work includes writing about the interaction of persons within society, such as *Civilization and Its Discontents* and *Totem and Taboo*.

This chapter attempts to use aspects of Freudian theory in the study of television's hard-boiled detective shows, such as "Magnum, P.I.," "Mannix," "Harry O," "Matt Houston," and, as a primary example, "The Rockford Files." Freud's theories concerning both the individual personality and society will be helpful in such an exploration.

In saying that the chapter will focus on the "hard-boiled detective," we make a distinction common in critical discussions of mystery fiction. The tales about private detectives are first distinguished from those about police detectives, such as "Barney Miller" or "Hill Street Blues," and spies, like "The Man from U.N.C.L.E." They then are divided into two groups, the *classical* and *hard-boiled* tales. The classical tales descend from the work of Edgar Allan Poe and Arthur Conan Doyle and include the work of writers like Agatha Christie and Ellery Queen. These "whodunit" tales are typically set among the upper classes and emphasize a puzzlelike plot complexity. Never particularly successful on television, attempts at the genre include "Nero Wolfe," "Ellery Queen," and "Checkmate." In contrast, the hard-boiled detective stories are more likely to feature a lower-middle-class American protagonist and to emphasize mood and action rather than the clearly developed resolution of mystery. Dashiell Hammett's Sam Spade and Raymond Chandler's Philip Marlowe are the literary forefathers of television's Joe Mannix and Jim Rockford.

Id, Ego, and Superego

In applying the Jungian model to science fiction, we suggested that, within a story, several characters might represent the striving toward wholeness of a single person. Thus, we identified the Self, the anima or animus, and the shadow. A similar approach can be made with Freud's discussion of the ego's struggle to balance the conflicting demands of the id and the superego.

It should be clearly understood that neither Freud nor the authors of this book understand the id, ego, and superego to be actual entities within the unconscious. They are not separate, willful beings. Rather, for Freud, they were ways of illustrating the powerful forces that shape our unconscious life. We suggest that these same concepts may be used to examine a narrative, to the extent that it expresses the same forces that Freud observed within the personality. Further, if these same forces are active in our own personalities, they may, in part, be responsible for gratification we receive from the narrative resolution of these conflicts.

The id is that impulse of the unconscious which expresses raging desire. The id knows no bounds and is unable to delay gratification. The id desires all things and does not want to be subjected to the constraints of reality. The id wants all pleasures, even when such pleasures conflict with each other. For example, the id wants the pleasures of both company and autonomy, of the mountains and the seashore, of sweet food and salty. Freud suggests we are all id at birth.

Though we may begin life totally subject to the irrational demands of the id, we cannot remain in such a state. As our perceptual systems develop and we come to relate cause and effect, the ego grows and is strengthened. The ego is the rational and reasonable portion of the unconscious. It gradually takes much of the place of the id, but the ego never completely frees itself from the id's demands. The ego has no energy of its own; it is fueled by the id's energy and strives to organize and satisfy the irrational strivings of the id. The decision to attend college, for instance, can be seen as an example of the ego limiting and channeling the id's demands. The id says, "I want gratification now"; the ego replies, "Wait four years," for a presumably greater gratification.

There is another force within the unconscious which bears down upon the ego. Freud calls it the superego. The superego is related to the idea of conscience, for it is an internalized moral authority. Like the ego, the superego develops in childhood. The very young child who obeys only when the parental authority is present is free of the constraint of the superego. But, just as each of us must develop an ego, so we develop a superego.

Freud traces this development, using a male model, through his discussion of the Oedipal crisis. Since the mother is the main source of pleasure for a young boy, he desires to possess her. Soon, however, he comes to see his father as an immensely powerful rival for the mother's attention and affection. Ruled by the id, the boy wishes to destroy the father; but his ego realizes the power of the father and fears him. The child's response to these conflicting emotions is to internalize the father and to identify with him and his power. This internalized authority figure is the superego. Though the internalized authority is based upon the external authorities whom the individual experiences, it is a harsh and punitive parody of the external authority. Unlike the parent or teacher, the superego is constantly present and punishes, not only the actual transgression, but the desire to transgress as well. It is the superego's power to punish the desire as well as the act that leads to our experience of guilt.

There is a third pressure upon the ego: the pressure of external reality. Thus, the rational center of the self, the ego, may be seen as a juggler who must constantly balance three powerful forces:

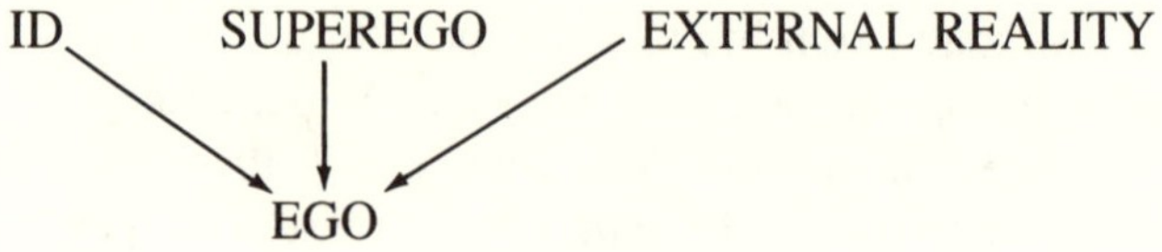

When the ego fails or comes near to failing to balance the three forces, anxiety is produced. Pressure from the superego produces moral anxiety. Pressure from the id produces anxiety about our powers and possessions. Pressure from the external world produces what can be called realistic anxiety.

The ego develops a variety of defense mechanisms to protect us from anxiety. These defenses may deny or alter reality in order to allow the ego to cope with internal needs. In this way, our fantasies are generated. At other times, the ego may identify with the threatening force or displace the anxiety so that our feelings are acted out, not on the forbidden object, but on some other, less protected object.

The goal of psychoanalysis is to strengthen the ego so that it can better juggle the forces that bear upon it. The well-developed individual will make little use of the superego, because the strengthened ego is strong enough to control the id rationally.

Applying the Model

In applying these ideas to a television detective story, we can begin by identifying our central character with the ego. Thus, in looking at "The Rockford Files," we can see Jim Rockford (James Garner) as an ego attempting to balance the pressures the narrative brings to bear upon him. Jim begins the tale in a rational, ego control of his life. Each case creates a state of anxiety in which one or more of the pressures upon him attempts to gain ascendency. The tale ends when the pressures upon Jim's ego are relieved and he regains a healthy ego control over the forces that have come to bear upon him.

In Freud's model, these forces are all within an individual unconscious, and, if we were interested only in the protagonist, we might attempt to psychoanalyze Rockford. While this can be attempted, it remains a problematic undertaking, since Jim Rockford is a fictional character and therefore has no unconscious to be explored except for that which has been made explicit in the tale.

What is attempted here is slightly different. Instead of psychoanalyzing Jim Rockford, we are using psychoanalytic theory to explore "The Rockford Files." If Jim is the ego struggling for rational control of his life, others represent the forces that bear down upon the ego.

The id finds two expressions in "The Rockford Files." Often, the criminal whom Jim faces can be described with the language we have used to discuss the id. The criminal is made up of uncontrolled desires. The criminal refuses to accept the limitation imposed by external authority and is motivated by the desire for immediate gratification. As an expression of the id, the criminal has no respect for others and attempts to use them for his or her own pleasures. Thus, Rockford's efforts to restrain the criminal and force him or her to accept the rational limitation of society parallel the ego's struggle with the id. In fact, in watching the show, we often find that Jim's ego-anger with the criminal is based, not so much on moral outrage as on what he sees as the basic unreasonableness of the antagonist's desires. A particularly amusing example can be seen in the episode that featured Rob Reiner as "King Sturdevant," a minor-league football player with an inflated self-appreciation. This totally self-centered id-figure draws Jim into a complex caper in which he becomes a quarry for both the FBI and the Mob. Rockford's greatest outrage is not directed at King Sturdevant's criminal acts or at the trouble they have. The worst thing, which Rockford has trouble believing, is that there is no reason why he has been involved. Sturdevant simply chose Rockford's name at random from the phone book.

Where the line is clearly drawn and the id is the *other,* as is usually the case when criminals represent the id, it is relatively easy for the ego to resist the id's demands. The id may be powerful and thus require a difficult struggle, but Jim is usually clear from the beginning that he intends to resist such demands. The complexity of the ego's struggle with the id is clarified in Jim's relationship to his sometime friend, Angel Martin (Stuart Margolin).

Angel is a personification of the id. He freely attempts to act out his desires, he readily takes advantage of Jim's friendship, and he is only constrained by the presence of outside authority or power. Like the id with which we have identified him, Angel experiences no sense of guilt and thus cannot restrain his passions in the absence of overt outside control.

Angel plays id to Jim's ego. Since they are connected by friendship, Angel's uncontrolled desires regularly make trouble for Jim. In one episode, Angel hires himself out as a hitman. He has no intention of actually killing anyone. As he explains to Jim, he will just take the "front money" and do nothing. Jim sees the danger in such a plan; but, in his attempt to extract Angel, Jim becomes identified with Angel and thus ends up once again pursued by both criminals and the police. It is a painful and difficult process; but, in the end, Jim regains control of the id by finding a rational explanation of the situation and undoing as much of the harm Angel has caused as possible.

The other two pressures on the ego present a problem with our application. How shall we distinguish between the pressures of the superego and those of external reality? In the psychoanalysis of an individual, this problem does not present itself, for the superego lies within the unconscious of the individual. When we apply these terms to individuals within a narrative, we must have some means of distinguishing between those who represent the superego and those who represent the pressures of external reality.

If we remember that the superego is a much harsher, more rigid reflection of the current social morality, some distinction becomes possible. Since Freud stresses the boy's relationship to his father, it is tempting to try to see Rocky (Noah Beery) as Jim's superego. But, in Freud's system, the superego is not simply the father internalized. Rather, it is the harsh, punishing, moralizing side of the father cut off from his other, more positive attributes. The superego only makes demands and punishes; it does not love and affirm. Therefore, for all the demands he makes on Jim, Rocky is not our superego.

"The Rockford Files" does feature a recurring superego figure. Freud tells us that the reasonably healthy ego makes relatively little use of the superego because it is able rationally to control the id. Rockford appears to be such an ego; but there is an irrational, distrusting moral force that comes to bear on him from time to time. The representatives of federal authority, particularly FBI agents, are presented on "The Rockford Files" in such a way that they make ideal representatives of the superego. Whenever Jim is forced to deal with them, they treat him with distrust and demand that he obey them without their offering him the information on which he could make a reasoned decision about the legitimacy of their demands. Often, Sergeant Becker's police superiors serve a similar function. They distrust Rockford and are suspicious of Becker's ties with someone who is not subject to their clear lines of authority.

In such a situation, the ego must struggle if it is not to surrender control to the irrational demands of the superego. Jim's weapon in these struggles is usually a dry wit. By poking fun at the superego's demands, he weakens its power over him. An example of this occurs in an episode in which Jim is forced to deal with an insurance adjuster who commands a National Guard unit on maneuvers. The man is obviously normally a quiet Milquetoast. Given authority, however, he becomes filled with self-importance and expects Jim to regard him with the same awe he has for his quasi-military role. When Jim deprecates the invasion drill the man is about to command, the insurance adjuster replies, "You won't think it's so silly when there is nothing between you and a horde of welfare cheaters but the National Guard." By this time, Rockford has freed himself from the superego demands and is able to respond, "Oh yes I will; I'm just a silly guy."

In addition to the irrational pressures of the id and superego, there are the pressures of external reality. The ego does not function in a vacuum. The physical world places certain restraints upon us, such as the limitations of gravity and physiology. Further, the existence of other people and the constraints of society, its laws, and its conventions limit the individual's options. Often, Rocky, Police Sgt. Dennis Becker, and Jim's attorney, Beth Davenport, serve to remind Jim of these outside pressures which must be acknowledged.

With the acknowledgment of the external constraints upon the ego, we are drawn to discuss society. Freud understood that the ego's balancing act did not take place in a vacuum. We are social beings; and, Freud would insist, as moderns, we are a particular kind of social being. Since the hard-boiled detective story takes place within the modern city, Freud's discussion of society should help us to flesh out our discussion of "The Rockford Files."

Freud's Social Theory

Freud saw modern society as the product and enforcer of rationality. While his system is clearly committed to the supremacy of reason, he is aware of its limitations and of the difficulty in maintaining rational ego control over the raging forces of the id and the superego.

Freud assumes that we are essentially self-centered. Each of us values his or her own pleasures above those of others; and, if we were free to pursue the desires of the id, we would use others for our own ends. Further, his model of happiness is the orgasm, the brief burst of relief, rather than that of lasting contentment. According to Freud, the reason we do not simply take our pleasures, sexual and otherwise, from others regardless of their willingness is that society is powerful enough to constrain us. For Freud, the democratic claims of equality and solidarity are not our deepest feeling: we actually regard ourselves as superior to others and consider it appropriate that our needs and desires come before anyone else's. However, we fear that others more powerful than ourselves will exact their pleasures at our expense and that society will punish us for taking our pleasures wherever we choose. Therefore, to protect ourselves, we conspire in a shared "reaction formation," in which we redirect our actual feelings to the opposite extreme. Thus, the claim of equality is fueled by the desire to be the unique center of the universe.

Although society is the servant of reason, an end Freud values, nevertheless, any society is the cause of much unhappiness. In order to constrain the individual, civilization turns the superego inward on behalf of society. Since the superego is strengthened by activity, the more civilization we have, the more guilt we will experience.

Since we are powered by the id's aggressive instincts, we will seek ways to displace the aggression we feel in some socially acceptable way. As civilization advances, it increasingly limits the acceptable expressions of aggression. Outlets for aggression that were acceptable in the past—both organized events such as the Roman circuses and bare-knuckles boxing, and informal expressions such as violence against racial or ethnic minorities—become unacceptable. Thus, modern society requires an unusual degree of instinctual renunciation, which inevitably leads to pain and alienation.

Society has mechanisms other than force by which it constrains individuals. Group life can be exciting and rewarding; but, Freud suggests, it can also be a kind of regression in which the leader serves as a substitute father-figure performing the higher functions that are normally internalized. Intellect, morals, and, finally, conscience become externalized. In this, Freud himself can be seen as proceeding much as we have here, for the leader becomes a kind of combination ego and superego for the group. In a similar way, Freud sees religion as a universal obsession by which a people create a shared defense mechanism and constraint that integrate them into society.

Since modern culture is highly developed and complex, it is constantly with us. The degree of instinctual renunciation required along with the guilt created by the strengthened superego of the modern person creates a modern people who are uniquely unhappy.

Any good critical system ought to be applicable to a broad range of narrative genres. So it is with our model drawn from Freud. However, it does seem that Freud's understanding of society lends itself particularly well to our discussion of detective fiction. The hard-boiled story, with its urban setting and gritty conventional realism, can also be seen as an exploration of how difficult it is to live within society.

Having arrived at a general theoretical outline, we will now attempt to apply it in a discussion of a particular episode of "The Rockford Files."

A Specific Application of Social Theory to Rockford

The episode of "The Rockford Files" entitled "Hazard" was written by Juanita Bartlett and directed by Jackie Cooper. It begins, like all episodes, with Jim's answering device receiving a phone message. These calls invariably bring bad news. His bookie may call to say that Jim owes money on a bet, or the laundry may call to say that his shirts have been delivered to the wrong address. In every case, the device that is supposed to simplify and enrich our life in society turns on Jim, bringing some constraint or misfortune to bear on his life. So it is in "Hazard"; the phone rings, and Jim's voice responds, "This is Jim Rockford. At the tone, please leave your name and number; and I'll get back to you." The caller responds, "Jim, I'm really sorry. I tried to catch you; that rally in Mexico that I told you about—it was yesterday." The calls have no direct relationship to the plot; they are attached randomly. What they do is establish the setting and define Jim's relationship to society. The phone call, like the fact that Jim lives in an aging mobile home at the beach, communicates the sense that here is someone at the edge of society who experiences its exasperating imposition and few of its rewards.

The "Hazard" episode begins in the office of Jim's attorney, Beth Davenport. Beth is seeing a stockbroker named Bailey who has been charged with tax evasion.

Bailey is called away to a secret meeting at "the usual place." There, a man named Metcalf warns Bailey that "Jordan found out" some undisclosed secret. Bailey rebuffs him and we see Metcalf leave the meeting, only to be captured by two hoodlums working for Jordan.

Rockford, fishing, is interrupted by his father, Rocky, who wants

Jim to go with him to look at a semitrailer rig for sale. Rocky, a retired trucker, is obviously caught up in the romance of becoming a trucking tycoon; and Jim tries to make him think logically about such an investment. Before they can leave, Beth calls to say that she has been jailed for contempt of court and wants Jim to bring her an envelope she needs from her office safe.

At Beth's office, Jim is attacked by the two men who picked up Metcalf. They empty the safe, taking, among other things, the evidence Metcalf had hidden there.

Rockford reports the attack to police sergeant Dennis Becker, and the two of them go to see Beth in jail. There, they find that she has been transferred to the prison ward at the hospital after having been poisoned.

Beth tells Rockford and Becker she had been allowed to see her client, Bailey, and the matron brought poisoned coffee. Because Bailey did not drink any of the coffee, Rockford suspects him, although Beth believes the poison must have been meant for her client.

Beth's professional discretion makes both Sergeant Becker's and Rockford's investigations difficult. Although she tells them for whom she was holding papers, she insists that the details of these papers are privileged information. When Becker and Rockford learn Metcalf had papers in the safe, Jim goes looking for him. But after forcing him to tell them about the evidence hidden in Beth's safe, Jordan's henchmen killed him, and Jim discovers the body. Metcalf was a union official who had charge of pension funds, and Jim suggests to Sergeant Becker that Metcalf could have been involved in skimming from the profits. If so, the missing papers might be evidence Metcalf had used to protect himself from his partners.

Rockford picks Beth up when she is released, but they are tailed by the two hoodlums. Jim causes enough commotion that they and the hoodlums are arrested.

After their release, Jim takes Beth to stay with Rocky. Throughout these adventures, Rocky has continued to want to buy the truck, and Jim has had to convince him to postpone the trip again and stay with Beth.

Bailey's bail-bondsman tells Rockford that Bailey, who has disappeared, may be staying with his (Bailey's) mistress. Rockford goes to her apartment, but is spotted there by another of Jordan's men.

Rockford accuses Bailey of complicity in Metcalf's death. When

James Garner in ''Rockford Files.''

Bailey flees, Rockford knocks him into the apartment pool. Bailey admits that he and Metcalf were stealing some of the profits from the union's stock investments. He says that Jordan, a mobster who controls the union, had Metcalf killed.

Jordan and his man arrive and Rockford and Bailey are ordered into Jordan's car at gunpoint. Jim manages to grab the wheel and force the car into the pool.

The episode closes with Jim and Beth at the beach. The police have Bailey and Jordan. Rocky arrives to tell Jim that it's all right that they didn't go see the truck since he has learned it was junk. Jim is relieved that Rocky seems over his dream of being a trucking magnate; but Rocky tells him, "There's this one I heard about over in Lancaster."

The Freudian model we have proposed can be applied to the "Hazard" episode of "The Rockford Files." It will be helpful if it gives us some insights into how to understand the interaction of the characters and the implication of the plot.

We might begin by noting that Jim does not have a client. His motives are personal rather than professional. This is a common occurrence in "The Rockford Files." In this, we see that, due to bonds of affection, Jim attempts to make life fair for someone. He is motivated by personal interest to try to force society to behave justly toward Beth. The fact that he lacks a client also means that Jim won't be paid. This parallels the many episodes in which he seems in the end to have earned a large fee or won a valuable reward only to have it denied on some technicality. Such events maintain Rockford's place as a marginal member of society. Society viewed from a Freudian perspective can be divided into two groups; those whose social positions and power allow them to enjoy society's rewards and those who must suffer the constraints of society without any realistic expectation of reward. Rockford's home in the trailer on the beach exemplifies both his remaining a have-not and the independence that status affords. Rockford can maintain a distance from society that limits the constraints upon him and allows him some simple pleasures. However, each case requires that he enter society in ways that inevitably must anger those in power.

It may be a sign of the difficulty the individual has in affecting society that, in this episode, events are clearly under way before Rockford becomes aware of them or involved. The tale begins in Beth's office, thus establishing a tenuous link with Rockford. Society is made up of powerful forces that inevitably reach out and affect us and those we love. The price of Jim's affection for Beth is that he is drawn into her affairs and is unable to remain indifferent to the forces that come to bear down upon her.

The bonds of affection that tie Jim Rockford to Beth Davenport are paralleled by the bonds of power and complicity that tie Bailey to Metcalf and connect them both to Jordan. Beth's link with Bailey is a socially proper one: she is his attorney. However, even socially sanctioned relationships exact a toll, and so Beth is punished by society for valuing her attorney-client relationship more than her relationship to the court. In addition, she is threatened by Bailey's and Metcalf's enemies, since she may know their secrets. In all this, Bailey, Metcalf, and Jordan may by seen as id figures. Their willingness to profit at the expense of Metcalf's union members is evidence of the id's power to convince us that our own desires are more important than those of others. These are not the obviously mad persons who often represent the id. In their apparent rationality, they reveal the id's ability to protect itself by taking on the outward appearance of the ego. They appear to be honest businessmen who conform to the rules and limits imposed by society. However, when Bailey meets Metcalf in secret, we see that this outward respectability is a mask that hides the id's unwillingness to be constrained.

When Rockford is introduced, we find him at the beach, fishing and oblivious to the powerful forces that will soon engulf him. He is joined by his father, who makes a demand Jim regards as unreasonable. In "Hazard," Rocky fills the role often taken by Jim's friend Angel. Rocky's desire to buy a semitrailer is a relatively harmless expression of the id's desires; and Jim clearly understands the proposal to be the request of his father's inner longings rather than a rationally considered business proposal.

This episode has the dual expression of the id that is common to "The Rockford Files." There are the criminals who represent the id in all its tragic power. They are paralleled by someone close to Jim who represents a comic expression of the id.

This dual presentation of the id has its parallel in the dual experience of constraint that follows it. Jim receives Beth's phone call and learns that she has experienced the repressive power of society. Her imprisonment for contempt of court might be described in terms of the superego, but it is probably better understood as a legitimate expression of the power of society. Jim's conversation with Beth is followed by a scene in which Jordan arrives at the place where Metcalf is being tortured. There can be no mistaking this harsh, punishing authority. Jordan may be an id figure in terms of his own desires for power and wealth, but his position as the representative of organized crime makes him a superego figure in his relationship to Metcalf.

These two punishing forces are given extreme expression. Society uses its power to imprison Beth. Jordan, the id figure, has Metcalf beaten and killed. After the story line has established that these powerful forces exist, they are next turned onto Rockford. The hoodlums beat Jim at Beth's office. He reports this to his police contact, but Sergeant Becker's first response is annoyance that Jim cannot better identify his assailants. Later, Becker will attempt to impose his authority by ordering Jim not to interfere in what is a police matter.

The visit to Beth in the hospital reiterates much that we have already established. Beth's condition is a reminder of the powers involved. Her unwillingness to divulge the nature of the papers she held for her clients, even though one of them may be involved in the attempt on her life, reminds us of the constraints and responsibilities of holding a place in society. Even in her weakness, Beth cannot escape being an attorney and the responsibilities that accompany that role.

The ego desires to meet our needs rationally. The attack on Beth causes Jim anxiety, and (although this is not made explicit) we assume that he wishes to look good in her eyes and therefore desires to solve the mystery of the attack on her. In doing so, he performs the ego function of restraining the superego's efforts to punish and the id's striving to possess whatever it desires.

Jordan is a powerful id figure. His desire for wealth and power is great; and, as an id figure, he experiences no inner limitation upon his striving. Therefore, when Beth is released from the hospital, his two hoodlums are waiting. They are not acting on their own, they should be seen as the strong arm of the id. Rockford spots them; and as is typical of him and as confirmation of the appropriateness of naming him the ego, his defeat of the id's attack is not a physical triumph. Rather, Rockford outsmarts them by tricking them into a situation where the police must intervene. In this way, the ego marshals the power of external reality against the raging of the id.

When Jim takes Beth to stay with Rocky, we are reminded of the id's more comic expression. Rocky is still anxious to pursue his truck-buying desire, and Jim must convince him again to postpone his trip and stay with Beth.

The fact that Bailey cannot be found confirms Rockford's suspicions. His rational pursuits by this time allow him, not only to suggest a link between Bailey and Metcalf, but also to find where Bailey is hiding.

Jim confronts Bailey and accuses him of complicity in Metcalf's death. The id never willingly accepts the ego's restraint, and so Bailey strikes Jim and flees. Jim pursues and restrains him by knocking him into the swimming pool. Finally overcome, Bailey explains how he and Metcalf had defrauded the union and blames Jordan for Metcalf's death.

The weaker id has been contained by the ego, but Jordan arrives to direct a fresh onslaught against the ego. He and his gunman force Jim and Bailey into a car. In a move that comically duplicated his earlier defeat of Bailey, Rockford seizes the wheel and steers them into the pool. This sudden bath gives Jim a final victory over the criminal id. He has solved the crime and saved Beth.

The closing scene on the beach wraps up the loose ends. We get a final explanation of the ego's victory over the criminal raging of the id. Rockford is returned to the beach, where we found him. There, the ego can rest and celebrate its victory over the forces that have come to bear upon it. Beth's presence may be understood as an implicit reward for his efforts. However, lest we think that the id has been forever defeated, Rocky appears, having located another used truck for possible purchase. The moment is comic, but the comedy rests on our acceptance of the never-ending demand of the id to be satisfied.

In all this, we do not, of course, suggest that the producers of "The Rockford Files" set out to illustrate Freudian theory. Rather, we believe that the Freudian understanding of the personality and of society can profitably be applied to the study of television shows and that such an application will enrich our viewing and sensitize us to the nature of the interaction between the characters and our relationship to the fantasy that we experience as viewers. The psychological tensions within the narrative embody pressures that each of us must balance within our own unconscious life. Thus, the narrative's suggestion of an at least temporary ego victory allows us vicariously to enjoy the resolution of tensions inherent in our life in the world.

part four

SOCIOLOGICAL AND ANTHROPOLOGICAL APPROACHES

The historical and structural approaches to television genre described in part two of this book concentrated on the *object*—the show or series and the structures that we, as critical viewers, suggest can be seen within these shows. In those chapters, we examined some of the *evolution of the forms* and formulas and the patterns that we observed and that we believe have meaning for us within the popular genres. The third part, on psychological approaches, emphasized the *effect of forms* on us as individuals, an effect on our psyches and behavior.

This part emphasizes the concept of *shared meaning*, effect, not on individual psyches, but on the American culture's—perception of itself as we see this perception presented in the fantasy world of television. This part focuses on three sociocultural problems: the belief in news as history and reality; the social impulse to categorize and simplify the "other" (in this case the ethnic other); and, finally, our society's perception of the very box, the television set, through which we get all the generic information. In short, in this part, we look at: (*a*) some social and anthropological implications of our video assumptions about reality; (*b*) the myths of television genre about those with whom we share our society; and (*c*) the television set that serves as mediator and medium for bringing us so many of our social concepts.

It is also important to point out that the three analytical sections of the book are not mutually exclusive, nor, we repeat, are they exhaustive. Our approaches are but examples of some of the ways of exploring television as a conveyor of genre. Each approach or series of approaches overlaps the others. Sometimes the overlap is great; so, it becomes difficult to exile psychological considerations from historical or social approaches, or, conversely, it is difficult to exclude from a consideration of psychoanalysis the social and historical background of a show, a series, or the medium of television itself.

Too frequently, we assume that approaches must be exclusive, that one discipline cannot or should not overlap the territory of another. Our position is, essentially, that the disciplines and approaches, as valuable as they are, were created by people as tools to understand themselves, their society, their universe, and the very meaning of existence. The tool must remain that, a tool, if it is to be of value. The approach cannot be the end in itself.

The reader may ask whether the chapters within part four, "Sociological and Anthropological Approaches," belong within a book on television genres. Though at first problematic, these approaches help to set our study of specific genres in a broader context.

Though television news is not usually thought of as a genre, we have approached it with the same questions we asked of clearly narrative genres: Why are we drawn to this material? and Why is it organized in the way that it is? Hopefully this application will encourage the reader to consider applying the idea of generic convention to other television forms that are not clearly narrative, such as sports broadcasting, or magazine feature shows, such as "Real People" and "That's Incredible!"

The other two approaches in this part move from the discussion of a specific genre. This reflects in part the tendency of social science approaches to focus more clearly on the relationship between the medium and the audience than on the internal structures of the narrative. The question of the presentation of specific ethnic images is an obvious place to examine the media's expression of social attitudes, and it requires us to work across generic lines. Readers with an interest in the presentation of a particular ethnic group may find it helpful to look for differences and similarities in several genres. Finally, in "Television: The Evil Eye," Dennis Giles and Marilyn Jackson-Beeck reverse our approach and, rather than studying television's assertions about society, examine our projections on to the medium.

So, to repeat our statement from the beginning of this book, we do not believe that there is a single correct interpretation or answer to the question of what is meant by a particular show, series, or genre . . . or the television set itself. There are a variety of explanations and explorations, each of value to the extent that the position or argument given is convincing, provocative, or meaningful to you as a reader.

—12—
Myth and History and Television News

Television news creates the reassuring, but essentially false, impression that a real world exists beyond us and our television set which can be wrapped, packaged, and understood like breakfast cereal and toothpaste. What the television news people are selling is an organizing entertainment and mythology under the respectable guise of "reality." There is nothing evil in what they are doing. It is not a terrible conscious or unconscious plot in the mode of *Network*. The worshiping of reality as seen in the news format of television is a social phenomenon we have engaged in for decades.

In an increasingly pragmatic world, we—and our media—have placed an ever higher priority on something we label "reality." At the same time, "fantasy" has been given less and less importance. Put another way, in dealing with the world, we have placed most of our trust in a belief in the primacy of the conscious world and have devalued the unconscious as an interesting but troublesome necessity we would prefer to be without.

This impulse toward the external world has led us, perhaps quite naturally, to a belief in history and the truth of history. People speak of history as if it were a self-evident teacher, as if there were some obvious order out there that we could pick up and examine and from which we could learn. We assume that history is irrefutable. It has already been observed, processed, and laid out in packages (books) like Kraft American cheese slices. All one needs to do is pick up the right one and swallow a truth.

In fact, the accumulation of our past is a massive and unorganized mess. Each day compounds the problem. Each day, a new series of infinite and related events takes place, of which we can absorb very little. Constant imaginative activity is required on the part of historians, newscasters, and others to create an order that makes events understandable.

Myth and History

Ideas about myth and history may help us to understand the relationship between historical events and how the events are organized and presented on television. Often, people assume myth and history are separate and opposite categories: history is supposedly real and tangible, while myth is fantasy. Or: history refers to those events that we know occurred, while myth refers to fanciful events that other people imagine to have occurred. In such a system, mythology becomes a way of talking about what other people believe.

However, as Mircea Eliade begins *Myth and Reality*:

> For the past fifty years at least, Western scholars have approached the study of myth from a viewpoint markedly different from, let us say, that of the nineteenth century. Unlike their predecessors, who treated myth in the usual meaning of the word, that is a "fable," "invention," "fiction," they have accepted it as it was understood in the archaic societies, where on the contrary, "myth" means a "true story" and, beyond that, a story that is a most precious possession because it is sacred, exemplary, significant.

A myth is a story that explains our origin, that tells us who we are by highlighting a mythic moment in the past when things came to be as they are, or, used less precisely, a paradigmatic moment that illustrates social meaning. Viewed in this way, myth becomes a helpful means of discussing those tales in which our culture has a continuing interest regardless of their historicity. For example, when we talk about the Western, there was indeed a Wyatt Earp, and one can go back to find what happened in Tombstone involving the Clantons and the Earps. But if one goes back to look at the historical data on the gunfight at the O.K. Corral, it becomes clear that what "actually" happened has very little to do with the particular Western mythology that has grown up around Wyatt Earp and that event. The lack of historicity has greatly concerned some people, who then expend a great deal of energy arguing that "It wasn't really like that!" Students of mythology have replied that our interest in such stories is worthy of study in its own right.

As E. H. Carr says in his book *What Is History?*, we labor under the delusion that history tells us something, that events speak for themselves. In truth, it is humans who decide, select, arrange, and attempt to make sense out of events. If we wait for history to tell us something, we will wait forever and in vain.

News Selection and Mythology

The reality of history and its most popular contemporary chronicle, television news, is that events are selected from the tangible world on the basis of a mythology, a set of beliefs we supposedly share about what is important. Those events are not only selected on the basis of this mythology, but they are presented and interpreted by performers to confirm and to conform with our mythologies. In a sense, it may not be reality that controls how we think about daily events; it is probably mythology that controls how we look at reality. We are simply under the illusion that it is the other way around.

The above argument is not made as a harangue against the media or an attempt to alter or reform news coverage and presentation. Indeed, it is unlikely that most of us would run the television news presentation differently from the way it is now run. We are part of the same culture and mythology. It exists and gives meaning and form to our experience of the outside world.

An essential point is that we exist under the illusion that the external world is somehow more real and important than the world that exists in our minds. We label the world outside our bodies "real" and treat it with respect. The world inside our bodies, our minds, is no less "real." We spend no less time experiencing it. In fact, we may spend *more* time concerned with the internal fantasy world, the unconscious, than we do with the conscious. An ideal state would probably involve a recognition that conscious and unconscious are not easily separable into categories of "reality" and "fantasy" or "history" and "mythology."

Viewing the evening, nightly, or even morning news is not simply a matter of sitting back and absorbing an encapsulation of the essential and relevant reality of the day. Viewing the news is a participatory act in which we are asked to agree with a particular set of mythologies. The ultimate goal, perhaps, should be not to get rid of the myths, but to understand them so that we recognize that they influence, alter, and determine what "reality" we will look at and what we will make of it.

Television news is presented in specific, highly structured form. There are one-hour news shows and half-hour news shows. Immediately, our organization of the day into hours affects how much time will be devoted to a particular presentation. The news must be made to fit in half an hour or an hour. Commercials cut the time down to about twenty-four minutes and forty-eight or fifty minutes. Within those time slots, there is already a predetermination of how events of the world will be divided. The news must fit into particular categories: weather, sports, editorial, human interest, etc.

While the format can change a bit, the conventional categorization is:

International news	Disaster; international relations
National news	Disaster; political; criminal; economic; public personas
Local news	Criminal; political; disaster; economic
Weather	Local; national
Sports	Local; national; personalities
Entertainment	Events; personalities
Editorial	Comment (almost always political, economic)

There is a rather clear generic context to each of the categories. International news, for example, is strongly tied to ideas of the epic genre. The death of fifty Nigerians in a plane crash would usually not make the television news in the United States, but a collapse of the Nigerian government and a takeover by the military fit our expectations of third-world events. International news must either present the epic condition of grandeur and spectacle—the major disaster—or the immediacy of war to have any great interest to an American television audience.

Occasionally, complaints are heard that television does not prepare us for the epic surprise. Afghanistan was a mystery until an American was killed there and the Russians invaded. Few Americans had heard of Grenada until U.S. Marines landed there. Voices of protest arose.

Why didn't we know? Why didn't the nightly news prepare us? Why did it have to wait until someone started a war? The answer, at one level, is simple. In the infinity of data of each day about each country, there was no generic context for dealing with the problems of Afghanistan or Grenada. There was no potential for understanding or being interested if one was not either deeply concerned or a political scientist. The problems of the third world had no mythic meaning until they focused in an understandable context: assassination, war.

In our generic understanding of the epic, there is a right and a wrong side in war. If this generic image is violated or questioned, the mythological order is threatened. Even in Vietnam, the epic assumption was accepted. It wasn't possible for the media and the public to consider that neither side was right or wrong, that there were different priorities and interests at work. Either the United States was good or it was evil. Mythologies are based on such clarity, and the media continue them as an abbreviation for understanding. The television news does not tell what happens in Afghanistan, Iran, or El Salvador; it presents a series of conventional statements and pictures that the audience can understand and categorize. A strike in Poland is presented as a prelude to a Spartan rebellion against Communism instead of a complex economic response, of which the Communist context is one element.

The hostage situation in Iran became a major embarrassment to television. The question was presented in epic proportions: Will this turn to tragedy? Triumph? Will this be a Great Escape, a Rescue at Entebbe? We had a villain, the Ayatollah; and the American government seemed to be in a perfect position to act as hero. However, heroism in this epic confrontation required invasion and action. We have no other epic response to such a situation. President Carter was presented as potential hero, as Gordon of Khartoum or MacArthur in the Philippines; but the tale went wrong. The mythological context was wrong. The potential satisfying scene of classic confrontation—heroic Americans rescuing innocents from fanatic foreigners—did not take place. The situation refused to conform to the mythology, and the television media seemed unable to change the mythological script. By day 400, the Americans were still prisoners; but the television news had exhausted the possible narrative. There was nothing to say. We simply waited for the tale to fulfill itself, waited for history to confirm mythology, expected that it would happen, knowing that the television news would guide events into an understandable mythic context.

A major problem related to the television coverage of events once they touch directly or are assumed to touch directly on the United States is the tradition of relating history to individuals. Ours, again, is a mythology involving people's supposed control over their own destiny. The image of Prometheus challenging the gods, David facing Goliath, or Perseus advancing on the Medusa can all be seen as mythic attempts to convert the historic actions of cultures to the image of individual action. The media are constantly asking the question, Who is responsible? It is not surprising, therefore, that for years Cuba got more coverage than Nicaragua. Cuba has Castro. Events in Nicaragua may have greater historical or political significance than those in Cuba, but Nicaragua has provided no mythic figure and so is more difficult for the television newscaster to analyze. In contrast, the "strong man" dictator is easier to categorize. Idi Amin's reign in Uganda was covered regularly. He was a villain of massive proportions, a shadow, a Hitler, a brother to the mad emperors of history—the abusers of power. At a time when events in Angola, Ethiopia, and Nigeria might reasonably have been judged more important to us than what was happening in Uganda, we heard nothing about these African states. There was no figure to categorize, to make responsible.

Social and historical analysis on television has not taken the form of analyzing the structures of race, sex, class, or economics that cause events. Rather, the news has given us mythic figures who represent both the current problems and more general hopes and fears for the audience. These individuals have not been seen as essential parts of an institution, an army, a corporation, or a conglomerate. They are the individuals who are *responsible*. This approach reflects the mythology that ours is a history governed by decisions of individuals, and not by social, cultural decisions. We keep getting rid of our leaders because they are failing to control destiny even though our system operates to limit the ability of leaders to control destiny. The news tends to confirm this mythology of individual-governed history.

Who is responsible? is the primary question for national news. This relates to popular culture figures as well as politicians and leads to inevitable cultural disappointment if the popular figure turns out to be unable to control destiny. However, the media, impelled by the public myth, tend to interpret actions as resulting in such control.

The mass media communicate powerful mythic images in which individuals come to stand for complex realities. This happens not only with political figures but with popular culture figures as well. These mythic images are not simply created by the media; the newscasters must respond to cultural forces. For instance, reporters and commentators initially responded with amused cynicism to the public response to Elvis Presley's death. But the popular media defer to the clearly expressed power of an image like Presley's, and the reporting on acts of public mourning and adulation have increasingly been reported with neutral respect.

One can go back to the beginning of news coverage in the United States and find people who were picked out as individuals to represent an ideal or image. There has had to be some sort of potential conflict, tragedy, or melodrama about their existence. If one doesn't exist, it may be created; and the selected individual may even accept and be destroyed by his or her mythic role (like Janis Joplin, Marilyn Monroe, or Freddie Prinz). We have almost no mythology about tranquil individuals. We won't see flamboyant features about Walter Cronkite or Dan Rather. The only time Cronkite or Rather becomes news is when they are in trouble or if they are involved in something that involves their mythic persona. In contrast to someone like Cronkite or Rather, the flamboyant persona lives out his or her tragic destiny.

On television news, we see individual foreigners only if they fit into some mythology we have about ourselves. We may suddenly discover that someone in another country has been very important for thirty years, affecting the destiny of millions. What happened in Iran is a good example. We knew nothing about Iran and its religion. We knew nothing about the religious structure, its relationship to politics, or the Ayatollah Khomeini. The revolution and its aftermath came as a shocking surprise to most Americans. Since it affected our image of who we are as a nation, we wanted to understand what had happened. At such times, we have floundered badly in dealing with Iran in the news. After the revolution, we first looked for a controlling figure. For months Khomeini refused to assume the role of the individual in control. There was the same problem with Nicaragua: the leftist rebels were unwilling to put forward a figurehead, and so they ceased to be in our news until the actions of the U.S. government provided a context within which to think about the Sandinistas. American television has to have a figure who can encompass a mythology, but there is a reluctance on the part of a Marxist organization to have such a figure, because it's really out of keeping with the model of a popular movement. Nicaragua is a

New York City Mayor Ed Koch being interviewed by Roger Mudd.

Edwin Newman reporting on location for a news special.

problem for the media: Castro came forth as a leader, as did Mao; but in Central America, the media has lacked such a mythic figure. Newscasters have been unsure whether to present guerrillas as heroic or villainous figures. Because of Yasser Arafat, the PLO gets a lot more attention than the other terrorist groups. Arafat is a person; he is a personality that can fit into a mythology.

Rarely does the news attempt to deal with change as a product of movements and ideas. For instance, the Chinese and Cuban revolutions are seen in the light of Mao Tse-tung and Fidel Castro. When Mao died, the media no longer knew how to report on China. The same problem will probably recur when Castro dies: if he *is* revolution, why doesn't the state collapse without him?

We have a problem in our country in reporting about inflation. The energy shortage created the model of the corporate villainy of the oil companies. Whether or not the oil companies were really doing dastardly things, we have gotten to the point where we have to have a villain. We have to have somebody or something responsible. OPEC or the Iranians are blamed, or the president of Mexico, or the oil companies. All of these beliefs may or may not be true, or all of them in combination may be true. These are complex issues; but to deal with the complexity ceases to allow the news to be compact and replaces the understandable mythic world with the potential world of chaos. So we tend to go with the mythologies that will "explain" events. It's better to blame problems on the "bad guys" and keep the evil "out there." If the villainy is elsewhere, we, of course, are not responsible. If the energy problem is the result of our consuming an unreasonable percentage of the world's resources, we must blame our own selfishness. Yet, we have no mythology for behaving selflessly. We've never had one nurtured in our media. So a governor or a president comes on television and says, "Drive a mile less today," and almost nobody does it. If a few people do it, they tend to be treated as fools, because our mythology does not applaud self-denial for the common good.

Sports news has long been related to the idea of a cult of personality. However, our beliefs about the motivation of sports figures have shifted radically. Where once we assumed they were primarily persons of dedication and integrity, we now have a new sports mythology about the importance of money, the importance of being a good businessman and of knowing one's worth. The shift has been particularly noticeable in the coverage of baseball personalities, and for a while, there was great media confusion about how to report on baseball. We had a transition period of about fifteen years in which the old announcers and long-time sports reporters wanted to see these new money-oriented figures as traitors to our mythical tradition. Sports in general, but particularly baseball, has been floundering for an image in the media.

Weather Reporter as Comic Relief

A disproportionate amount of news time is devoted to coverage of the weather. From a little tag item at the end of early television news, it has been expanded to take up a significant part of the alloted news time. The mythology of the weather, to a great extent, can be related to the idea of personality in the composition of the local news team. At the local level, it's fairly clear that the weather reporter usually serves as a kind of generic equivalent to the comic relief. Unless we have truly disastrous weather, the necessary information could usually be communicated in fifteen to twenty seconds. It could be printed on the screen: what the weather's going to be like tomorrow, all the data, even the barometer readings and what the weather is like in Louisiana. Anything else you wanted to include could be presented in fifteen to twenty seconds.

For a long time the use of women to report the weather caused problems because the stations did not understand what image their audience wished to see the weather announcer fulfill. The stations intended to give women a relevant role, not use them for comic relief. So there was the "weather girl" filling a comic time slot and not being funny. The stations had assumed that weather was an informational function rather than a mythical function. Gradually, as a familial mythology developed for the "news team," role models did evolve: the paternal anchor person and a younger "daughter" or "son" as co-anchor, a brash nephew for the sports or lovable uncle for the weather.

The weather person brings tremendous technology—barometers, satellite photographs, and government forecasts—to bear on a matter of relative unimportance. We cannot affect the weather, and, short of a disaster, it will have little effect on our activities. This creates a kind of ironic seriousness, for the weather person is presented as a wise person, a scientist, who knows something which is finally not very important. This paradox often leads to clowning. In Detroit, Sonny Elliot literally used to be a clown before he became the weather person. He made bad puns about the weather, and he came out wearing silly hats. On CBS in Chicago, the weather person tends to break out of the format and talk to the people about his private life. By being personal, rather than coldly scientific, he does not conform to what is assumed to be his limited role. He's an eccentric. The popularity of the weather person on television has tended to relate to his ability to mediate the role of the interesting eccentric with that of the scientist.

The News Team

For some time now, the emphasis of local news has been on having a news "team." Instead of an individual, there is a group that organizes the news to fit the myths. The intellectual, ethnic, and racial composition of news teams does not reflect the constituency with which they deal. Rather, the news team embodies mythological assumptions about what the power structure is in the community. Who would know things? What kinds of people have contacts? People of this sort are the primary figures on television news. Among street reporters who form the next-lower echelon, there is a greater variety of ethnic representation. There is a quite clear difference between the people who work in the studio and the people out on the street carrying microphones.

Chicago CBS news lacks a father figure. That news show has an institutional orientation without having the paternal figure. What has tended to happen, at least in Chicago, is that, when someone takes on the image of controlling father, his job comes into jeopardy.

There is also an interesting set on the Chicago CBS news. It is made to look the way CBS thinks people who watch television think a newsroom looks. It resembles the newsroom in "Lou Grant," which in turn looks like the *Washington Post* or some of the other larger newspapers. It is the image of a place where news accumulates. It might be more efficient to set the TV news up in some other way. But that image of the newsroom is important. You think you are seeing the things as they are happening. The mood and image are of a working situation, not a staged presentation.

One practice that's taking place increasingly in news is the sexual sharing of the news spotlight. A man and a woman co-anchor in a state of assumed parity. The stations do not know how to maintain this parity, because we have difficulty determining in a contemporary mass presentation what parity is or should be. And so, news items take on a hierarchical quality: a decision is made to flip a coin and say, "Oops, she's going to deliver this news, and he's going to deliver that other news." Or somebody has to determine what is a "male's story" and what is a "female's story." At some level, the image of the person delivering each piece of news will affect how people perceive that information. In order to organize their stories and presentation rationally, the producers of the news shows have to make assumptions about the mythologies of their audience concerning sexual images. It is easier to make such judgments at the local level than to generalize about mythologies of the entire nation.

To a great extent, what we live with is a world of chaos and confusion. What we get on television news is a kind of familial corporate image, a group of people who organize events into a mythically consistent order. These figures put events into perspective and balance the world by means of a traditional mythic history. Their function, whether familial or paternal, is to present events to us as governed by a traditional way of viewing that world. In other words, the news often presents a world governed by individuals with foibles and strengths that we can understand.

—13—
Ethnic Images in American Popular Culture: Revolution, Evolution, or Variation?

Popular media have, since their inception, tended to deal with people as types. This tendency is not a peculiar characteristic of American literature, film, radio, and television. It is shared by many peoples. The vast majority of the world's popular narrative works are dependent on a kind of shorthand relying on types which that particular culture recognizes and accepts.

The presentation of types is based heavily on what information the creators feel they must give their audience for the audience to recognize and feel comfortable or uncomfortable with a character. When we look at the changing images of minorities over a given period in literature, film, or television, we are really looking at what image of that minority the viewing public is willing to accept at a particular point in time.

Considerable work has been published on the presentation of Afro-Americans on television. There seems no reason to review superficially what is available in detail elsewhere. The reader is especially directed to J. Fred MacDonald's very thorough *Blacks and White TV*. Less critical attention has been paid to the images of other minorities, and a brief look at the presentation of a number of reoccurring ethnic types seems useful.

An examination of minorities in television over the past fifteen years shows a change in typing but not necessarily a step toward reality. Such an examination reveals how the majority fantasizes a minority, so that the majority can cope more easily with a group it does not understand. What we see is not what is forced upon us by an insidious industry but what is accepted as representing the type at a given point in time.

In order to make these ideas clear, it will often be necessary to rely on examples from popular films rather than television. This is not because television does not depend on ethnic typage to tell its stories—it does. However, most series make use of a parade of ethnic types that vary from episode to episode, so that it is difficult to suggest television examples with which the reader may be reasonably expected to be familiar. Where a television show has consistently made use of a particular type, we have taken it for an example. Otherwise, we have used film examples that should allow the reader to make the connection with similar presentations in specific episodes from television series. We will now consider the following ethnic types: Germans; American Indians; Irish; Italians; Jews; Latinos; Asians; Poles; Russians; and Scandinavians.

Germans

Germans in American films since World War I and in television have frequently been viewed as enemy or potential enemy. They are often seen either as highly intelligent, resourceful, and emotionless or as sadistic followers of orders. Thus, superior film villains such as Walter Slezak in *Lifeboat* and Maximilian Schell in *Counterpoint* along with television villains in "The Rat Patrol" and the Robert Goulet spy series "Blue Light," have their counterparts in the frequently bald, neckless sadists such as George Zucco in *The Seventh Cross* or Anton Diffring in *Counterpoint*. Put another way, media Germans are often (*a*) worldly and intelligent with an evil desire for power over those less capable than themselves or (*b*) subhuman sadists who perform the will of the intelligent superior but are ever on the verge of taking over.

The superior German in such a series as "Combat," "Tales of the Gold Monkey," "Bring 'em Back Alive" or "Casablanca" can be seen as the Nietzschean superman eventually destroyed by the more emotional, well-meaning American, Frenchman, Scandinavian, or Englishman. He has everything going for him but "goodness." The only thing we have between him and us is that he is wrong; were not God and the filmmaker on our side, the villain would triumph.

The intelligent German is much akin to the mad but powerful doctor or scientist in horror films. Quite frequently, as with Frankenstein, he is a German who works with a deformed and sadistic assistant. Humanity is threatened by the two of them, and they are defeated only by the hero who receives the hope of God. The German is presented as a pseudo-god who will suffer for such an affront to Western understanding of good and evil.

Clearly, all Germans are not treated this way; but this tendency, even when dealt with comically as in television's "Hogan's Heroes," indicates that the Germans still represent a kind of mad efficiency with a tunnel vision that does not permit them to consider the human consequence of their goals and drives. For example, the Germans existing in the microcosm of the club in *Cabaret* are unable to differentiate between what we as American filmgoers see as propriety and evil. Each of Joel Grey's numbers becomes more grotesque in its assumption of Germanic superiority over traditional concepts of good and evil.

American Indians

More has probably been written about the image of Indians than any other group except blacks. The primary problem of much of this writing is that it has simply chronicled and documented that American popular film has treated the Indian derisively, cruelly, and "unrealistically"—that, in short, film and television have been "unfair" to the Indian. We hardly need historical evidence to discover such data about Indians or any other group in American film.

The Indian has been traditionally presented in two ways, neither of which has much to do with reality. Since the days of James Fenimore Cooper, the Indian has represented either the noble savage (Tonto) or the mad animal (Geronimo). Such a polarity represents the attitude the American popular audience has toward the myth of the Indian, since in most parts of the United States, whites, blacks, or Oriental Americans encounter very few real Indians.

The Indian has been used as a symbol of a primary problem of American history. American films and television vacillate between veneration of "natural" humanity and fear of the "natural" state. Sometimes, the Indian is a brutal savage, an animal overcome by feelings, a painted, naked monster who must be destroyed. As such, the Indian has been metaphoric of the savagery of American history, the savagery and animalness of survival. Indians seen as savage in films or television series, such as "The Quest" or "How the West Was Won," are overcome by civilization, reason, and organization in the guise of white civilization.

The image of the animal-like savage Indian has existed side by side with the noble "natural man." Such an Indian—usually not played by an Indian at all—is presented as having virtues of nature. He is to be emulated for his naturalness which puts to shame the restrictions of civilization. Ed Ames played such an Indian in "Daniel Boone," as did Michael Ansara in "Broken Arrow." In "Ryan's Hope" on television, the antagonist to Frank Ryan is Seneca Beaulac, of Indian background. Yet Beaulac is also a hero. His major distinguishing deed was motivated by his supramoral natural instinct: he pulled the plug on his vegetable-comatose wife. He has in general been presented as a brilliant doctor (medicine man?), yet one open to excessive pride and emotional inspiration.

Irish

Until about forty years ago, the Irish filled the social slot occupied by blacks today: they were a feared media minority. Film criminals were Irish; murderers were Irish; crooked politicians were Irish. The relationship of such stereotypes to reality was relatively clear. The Irish were the primary urban immigrant population with a popular image of low education, aggressiveness, and hard drinking.

By the 1940s the Irish were rapidly being absorbed into society and replaced by other ethnic groups on the lower social rungs. Many of the Irish became urban politicians. To a degree, TV and film have reflected this transition. However, in film and television, the Irish politician can never escape his past or his background, and generally he does not want to. He retains his lower-class or Irish accent and his lower-class mannerisms. If he is intelligent, like Frank Skeffington in *The Last Hurrah* or Frank Ryan in the soap opera "Ryan's Hope," he plays on these mannerisms to indicate that he is a man of the people.

The Irish politician provokes an ambivalent reaction in American viewers. His aggression and resourcefulness are admired, but they can easily become criminal or lead him to ambition higher than "he should have" according to the myth of American order projected in film.

However, TV and film also feature the Irish hero, who differs from these coarse men of temper and violence. Like the villainous politicians, Irish heroes are headstrong; but unlike the politicians, they are not wily. Irish characters can be heroes particularly in a military tale that legitimates the image of the daring Irishman of the IRA. But, like heroes of several other ethnic groups, there is a level beyond which they cannot aspire. The Irish never attain filmic respectability. They serve only as intermediaries between the established order and the lower classes. The Irish are always on the verge of being assimilated, but, because of their Catholicism, which separates them from the general populace, they remain outsiders. This can be seen in films, such as *The Cardinal* and *Say One for Me*, and television series, including "Going My Way" and the short-lived "Kate McShane," in which Anne Meara played a defense attorney aided by her priest brother and ex-cop father. Here was the upwardly mobile Irishwoman supported by men who filled traditional Irish roles, reminding us of both their Catholicism and the combination of a paramilitary ideal with urban power-brokerage. In "Ryan's Hope," although members of the Ryan clan are the intermediaries between the poor and the rich, envied for their heritage and religion, they are outsiders. The rich Coleridge family, for instance, even define themselves in relation to the Ryans: none can be happy unless in the presence of a Ryan. The Irish culture itself becomes mythological; young characters who truly should have no accent at all speak the brogue that denies the American melting pot.

Frequently, the older Irishman in American film and television is seen as a nonthreatening, comic character, a near drunk with a red nose and a big heart. The Irishman's reward for being an intermediary between "us" and "them" is a mythic old age as comic retainer, a role frequently played in films of two decades past by Barry Fitzgerald and more recently by Art Carney in television's "Lannigan's Rabbi."

Italians

A case might be made that Italians appear more frequently in American popular film than any other ethnic group. In fact, like Jews, with whom they most often appear interchangeable, the proportion of Italian characters in American films far exceeds their representation in American society.

The Italian, perhaps more than any other ethnic group member, has represented a counterculture in American film, an alternate life-style and a challenging doppelganger. The Italian gangster makes a mockery of the American dream and social aspiration. His success or failure, from *Little Caesar* to *The Godfather,* mirrors the myth of the American dream. His accent and unwillingness to be assimilated into society keep him a threat.

The Italian gangster has been a regular feature in such television series as "Toma" and "Baretta." There, the gangster, who was usually played by an actor like Will Kuluva or Mark Lawrence, who had played heavies in the forties or fifties, confronts an Italian cop. The Italian who has aligned himself with society and its restrictions has a respectable but limited place in that society. He is contrasted with the gangster, who has attempted to have a greater place in society by circumventing its restriction. Such stories tell of the price the gangster pays for his presumption.

Perhaps most important, the Italian is presented as a creature of family. The family—whether the pseudo-family of the Mafia or gang or a conventional family in films such as *Made for Each Other* and *Lovers and Other Strangers* or in TV shows like "One Day at a Time," "Taxi," or "Ryan's Hope"—is central and all-consuming. The Italian constantly refers to it, and it is the family to which he or she remains loyal. The Italians of popular culture are presented as being emotional, giving love readily and responding violently.

This familial attachment and its attendant emotion can be presented as comic, as in films like *Lovers and Other Strangers* or *Made for Each Other,* and such television series as "Angie" and "Laverne and Shirley." It may also be tragic, as in *The Godfather, The Brothers Rico,* and television's "Honor Thy Father." Whether comic or tragic, Italian family ties are always in contrast to the less emotional, less intense family bonds of the WASP Americans depicted.

A major Italian character in "Ryan's Hope" was Jack Fenelli—whose general unhappiness results from his being an orphan who never had the traditional Italian values of family. A loner, he alternately goes to and recoils from the Ryan family as a substitute culture. His problems are portrayed as directly related to his turning his back on the "Italian" (and Irish) values: he functions as the exception that proves the rule.

The connection of Italians with emotionalism shapes the presentation of Italian women. Earthy, voluptuous (Sophia Loren, Gina Lollobrigida types), emotionally open and sensual, upon maturity they will turn into the older Italian women of the American media: supportive of their men, good cooks, caretakers of large families.

Jews

The entertainment media's dominant view of the Jew has not really changed greatly in the last three decades. As with all ethnic groups, there are a variety of types from which to choose. The primary negative image of the pious Jewish moneylender departed from the film as a central image long ago, although it reappeared in comic form in the affectionate guise of Fagin in *Oliver!*

Even when the Jew shed his beard, coat, stoop, and accent somewhere in the 1930s, he retained contradictory characteristics. Jews were and continue frequently to be identifiable by the fact that the males, even if not played by Jewish actors, are often slight, intelligent, self-interested, and highly emotional; for example, Montgomery Clift in *Freud,* Richard Benjamin in *Goodbye, Columbus* and on television's "He and She," Gabriel Kaplan in television's "Welcome Back, Kotter," and Joe Spano (Goldbloom) in "Hill Street Blues." With such characteristics, they are not suited in the fantasy world of radio, film, and television to positions of wartime leadership. They can provide comic relief or even sage human advice, since, like all ethnic minorities, they seem to have a wellspring of emotion that the majority whites in American films tap for renewed vitality.

Young Jewish women are invariably dark, security-seeking pragmatists like Rhoda Morgenstern from TV's "Mary Tyler Moore Show" and its "Rhoda" spin-off. This pragmatism may be tempered by their being politically or socially radical. The equation of Jew with Red has persisted in film and television from the early silent films until the present. It is possibly a variation on the idea of Jew as foreign element bringing either mystical or radical ideas from Europe.

Older Jews are slightly different. The Jewish mother persists; but, as in literature, she has become overpowering, oppressive. Her motivation is an ever-present drive for security, to be obtained either by having her daughter marry a wealthy man or her son become a member of a secure profession. The television series "Bridgit Loves Bernie" featured such a mother (Bibi Osterwold), and Gertrude Berg in the long-lived "The Goldbergs" was almost archetypal. The Jewish mother is like Bernice, wife of Fish on the TV show named for him. She is filled with energy and action—a person who draws attention to herself.

Her husband, in contrast, is like Fish: a man resigned. The Jewish husband in American film and television of the past three decades is a man who accepts the myth forced upon him by a Jewish mother. He has usually attained security via a trade or business rather than the profession his son will pursue. Secure, he alternates between questioning his life and being protective of what success has brought him.

The one major change in the image of Jews has possibly been a result of the emergence of Israel. Since the demonstration by Israel of its military ability, American films and television have added a new Jewish character; the resolute, tough man of principle (Paul Newman in *Exodus;* Cliff Gorman in *Rosebud;* George Peppard in *Tobruk;* Kirk Douglas in *Cast a Giant Shadow;* Robert Shaw in *Black Sunday*). Paul Michael Glaser in Starsky on TV's "Starsky and Hutch" was such a character. Other examples would be Timmy Siegel in "One Life to Live," a hotheaded law student in love with a Polish nun, and Hal Linden's title character in "Barney Miller." The man may border on the fanatic, but he is a man who demands the center of the screen.

Latinos

The evolution of Latin types in American media has been primarily from comic and cutthroat to avenger. The enduring Latino types include the comic buffoon—a dark, frequently fat, heavily accented man who poses no threat to the protagonist and can be endured by being laughed at. Examples in film are Chris Pin Martin in *Stagecoach,* Peter Ustinov in *Viva Max,* Gonzales Gonzales in *Rio Bravo,* and, in television, Leo Carillo's Pancho in "The Cisco Kid."

The Latino cutthroat has endured, at the same time undergoing a gradual transformation. The Latin bandit, from *The Treasure of the Sierra Madre* through *The Magnificent Seven,* has been a man of unpredictable violence, a man who often prefers the personal knife to the distancing gun. (Tony Franciosa in *Rio Conchos;* John Saxon in *The Appaloosa* and *Joe Kidd).* He is unkempt and frequently has many followers. Metaphorically, the Latin bandit embodies the fear in the urban Anglo community that Latinos will be dangerous and unclean and that they will multiply. In opposition to such bandits, an individual white arises or a group gathers together to wipe him out. *The Magnificent Seven, They Came to Dordoisa,* and *The Wild Bunch* are all examples of such tales. What they destroy is a way of life alien to that of the American stereotype.

The cutthroat image moved in the 1950s to the urban situation. The Latino became an urban bandit, still opposed by a white majority. In *The Young Savages, Touch of Evil, West Side Story,* and *Red Sky at Morning,* the urban fear becomes manifest. At the same time, an alternative to the myth emerged. The Latin began to be seen also as a man alone against a corrupt white society. He emerged as a potential believer in a political system that whites in the film have often abandoned. An almost prototypal example existed in the Anthony Quinn series "Man and the City." Such Latino protagonists are typed as resourceful, doggedly determined, and strongly dedicated to the principles of aspiration taught by American myth. Charlton Heston played such a Latino in *Touch of Evil;* Burt Lancaster, in *Valdez Is Coming;* and Marlon Brando, in *Viva Zapata*. Later, such Latinos appeared on television in "Chico and the Man," "Hill Street Blues," and the Gregory Sierra character in "Barney Miller."

It is true, of course, that such ethnic typologies do not simply disappear or evolve. Change is not that simple. The loathsome cutthroat continues to appear in American television alongside the heroic Latino. The types are placed in different contexts, their myths perhaps expanded or varied.

Asians

American distrust of Orientals was heightened during World War II, for Americans could not and would not differentiate between Japanese (our enemy) and Chinese (our ally). The lack of differentiation can be seen in the fact that American films frequently used Chinese actors as Japanese. Richard Loo and Phillip Ahn both became prototypal Japanese officers.

During World War II, the Japanese were seen as emotionless, cold, and sword-happy. The Japanese were the extension of the Mongol horde, the dreaded Yellow Peril. The Japanese were not human and did not understand love; they killed little babies (*Behind the Rising Sun*), and tortured innocent men (*The Purple Heart*), and enjoyed doing these things.

With the end of the war, the Japanese adapted quickly to American occupation, and a radical shift took place. Films dealing with World War II but made after the war emphasized the humanity of the Japanese which the American soldiers in the films overlooked (*Too Late the Hero; From Here to Eternity; Hell in the Pacific).*

Then, the Red Chinese became our enemy, and the negative traits we had applied to the Japanese were shifted on film and television to the Chinese and Koreans (*The Manchurian Candidate; The Chairman)*.

Though the nationality of the mistrusted Oriental group has varied over the years, the stereotype has remained. The mistrusted Oriental is isolated, difficult to trust or understand. Unlike the Jew, the Oriental is not depicted as a domestic threat. For one thing, like the black, the Oriental can immediately be identified and typed, cannot infiltrate society—though he can assault it.

Outside of war films and war television shows, Oriental men have been docile, accepting, and loyal. Jack Soo as Sergeant Yemena on "Barney Miller" was a comic extension of this idea. The women have been shy. They have, as types, been a protected group in American film as long as the story has an American setting. When the American is displaced into an Oriental setting, he is forced to confront the mystery of the Oriental. See, for example, various films concerning Marco Polo's confrontations with Kublai Khan (*The Adventures of Marco Polo; Marco the Magnificent*); or such diverse films as *The General Died at Dawn* and *The Barbarian and the Geisha*.

When Oriental characters are allowed to be heroes in American media, the character is generally played by a non-Oriental. For example, Charlie Chan in film was played by white actors Sidney Toler, Warner Oland, and Roland Winters. The same was true on television, where Chan was played by J. Carrol Naish and Marvin Miller. Both Mr. Wong and Mr. Moto were played in film by Occidental actors, Boris Karloff and Peter Lorre, respectively.

While martial arts films made in Hong Kong have achieved great popularity in the United States, variations made in the United States differ markedly. *Enter the Dragon* and *The Golden Needles*—or even *The Man with the Golden Gun*—place the Oriental martial artist in a position in which he is secondary to the white protagonist. In the television series "Kung Fu," the problem was solved by having a Caucasian actor, David Carradine, portray a Chinese, and in the more recent *The Master,* both the Ninga master and his apprentice are presented as Caucasians who make use of an Oriental skill and knowledge. However, even in Hong Kong films, the skills of the martial artist are directed, not primarily against whites, but against Orientals, much like the Mexican bandits of previous decades. Bruce Lee and his followers

Geoffrey Pierson and Malcolm Groome in ''Ryan's Hope.''

Julie Kavner, Valerie Harper, and Nancy Walker in ''Rhoda.''

take on great numbers of Oriental villains and defeat them before the villains can take over more territory or power or hurt more people. In his fury, Bruce Lee is diametrically opposed to the emotionless domestic Oriental.

Polish

The image of the Pole has remained essentially unchanged for decades. He is a kind of accented Frankenstein's monster: slow-witted, large-bodied, and friendly. He is seldom part of a decision-making process. He is like Wojo on "Barney Miller," the acceptable work force, the good laborer, the willing infantryman, the immigrant who will not threaten the majority. The Pole can aspire toward higher levels of participation in society; but we recognize by type that he will never achieve anything more than middle-management level.

That this may not conform to reality is not relevant. The Pole serves as a representative of the Eastern European. Eastern Europe poses no threat to the United States either mythically or physically—except for Russia, and Russians are presented differently. For example, the English have served as a class threat in American films; the French, as an emotional and cultural threat; the Italians, Germans, and Russians, as physical threat. The German threat has been external, while the Italian threat has been internal—in the idea of organized crime.

Poles, however, provide no threat of the kind indicated above, nor are they seen as providing input to American culture beyond the strength of their arms. A few exceptions have crept into recent television in the Rob Reiner character on "All in the Family" and the Wolek family in the soap opera "One Life to Live." One Wolek is a doctor, although another, a police officer, remains crude, muscular, and likable.

A possible alternative role for the Eastern European in the post–World War II period has been to portray animosity toward the Soviet Union. The recent struggles of the Solidarity movement, and the American response, make possible a, at least temporary, revision of the image of the Pole. Because Solidarity has been presented as a challenge to the Soviet Union, Poles have become potential heroes. This recasting of the image has already made Polish jokes socially unacceptable. It will be interesting to see what use is made by the media of the current Polish image.

Russians

Thickness has been the single identifying word for Russians in American films. The cold war and the thaw have done little to change this.

The Russian of popular culture is a bear—an uncivilized, cunning animal who has put on a coat, exerted his strength, and demanded that the world treat him as if he were human. Like a bear, the Russian must be treated carefully. He can be friendly, but he can turn and smother you suddenly. He can comically ride a circus bicycle one moment and claw you to death in the next.

The Russian in American film has been a man (very few Russian women appear in American films) who laughs easily and heartily and who can be clever but moves mentally and physically a little more slowly than his American counterpart. Where women have appeared, they have usually been presented as beautiful animals. They are spies kept by the government to tempt Westerners, as in *From Russia with Love*.

The Russian type likes coarse foods and simple pleasures. His variant came in the émigrés, the Russians who left before or during the revolution and who retained an aura of aristocracy in American films. Such Russians were indeed variants but not racially different. They were comic bears in ethnic garb, not quite passing as Western Europe aristocracy but doing their best, typed as doormen or waiters, wearing the mock uniforms of a fallen aristocracy. More recent Russians in American film have been more clever (*The Billion Dollar Brain; Scorpio; The Tamarind Seed*), but the earthiness and our fear of the earthiness remain.

Scandinavians

In American film (omitting those that deal with the Viking, who serves as the Grendelian demon) the Scandinavian has been pictured as the perfect immigrant, the ideal American newcomer. The Scandinavians are seen as reliable, God-fearing, and brave individuals who pose no immediate threat to the majority, because of their mythical commitment to America as an ideal. Inger Stevens as Katie Holstrum in the television series "The Farmer's Daughter" was nearly archetypal. Scandinavians cause no trouble, espouse no causes, and make perfect wives or husbands. The film *I Remember Mama* and the television series it led to form a case in point, and the title reinforces the happy memory of the myth.

The lack of dimension is just as clear in such media presentations as in those involving Poles or Russians. However, whereas the Pole can be seen as a kind of Frankenstein's monster and the Russian as a bear, the Scandinavian can be compared to one of *The Stepford Wives*.

Conclusion

While most depictions of ethnic groups tend to reduce the dimension of the individual portrayed, they do reflect and add to our myths of life and types. As our myths are ambivalent, so, often, are the ethnic characters presented in our films.

The attempt in film to deal with minorities by reduction to a type is found in all cultures where films are made. It is interesting, for example, to examine the portrayal of the American in British and Russian films. The process of typage seems inevitable. These presentations should be seen as revealing more about the dominant culture's projections than they do about the people portrayed. However, they also create obvious and regrettable problems for the human beings who find themselves reduced to types. Unfortunately, as attitudes about particular groups change, our negative projections may be displaced onto some third group, but the mythic function of the "other" seems inescapable. For example, the presentation of blacks and Hispanics may have become more positive in recent years, but at the same time, Middle Eastern, particularly Arabic, people have taken on many of the villainous stereotypes. The media Arab of today is either a murderous terrorist or an oil-exploiting sheik.

—14—
Television, the Evil Eye
by Dennis Giles and Marilyn Jackson-Beeck

This chapter concerns the fear of television, the suspicion of television—"videophobia." In the United States, a wide range of dire effects is attributed to television exposure. TV is popularly suspected to cause a kind of moral damage to the individual. It appears to encourage violent, destructive behavior. Sitting too close to the set may somehow damage the viewer's eyes. Children are believed to be the principal victims of television, because they have not yet learned to erect psychological defenses against its onslaught of images. Parents fear that their children will be "formed," or, rather, "deformed" by television and therefore must be protected against it, as the citizens' group ACT (Action for Children's Television) attempts to do.

Responding to these popular fears sometimes expressed through Congress, researchers have gathered scientific evidence concerning the dangers of television, most of which is summarized in the report to the surgeon general of the United States, *Television and Social Behavior.* Evidence concerning the effects of TV viewing usually is tentative, contradictory, and inconclusive, as Comstock, et al., indicate in *Television and Human Behavior.* Popular suspicions regarding the medium have rarely been fully confirmed—or firmly denied. But despite this, suspicion of television remains at large in the land.

Whether or not videophobia is justified by the empirical evidence, the fear of television is real. This fear is a cultural phenomenon, and, as such, a fit object of investigation for students of American culture. Here, we posit an *association* between the fear of television and an ancient, still powerful pattern of belief well recognized in the Old World. We suggest that videophobia reflects the same suspicions as stem from that phenomenon known as the *evil eye*. Just perhaps, the suspicion that harm will result from exposure to the electronic "eye" of television is a displacement and *re*-presentation of the fear that the gaze of a specific person has the power to seize, destroy, sicken, or otherwise ruin an animal, a prized possession, or especially *a child*.

Our argument is developed in three stages:

1. We cite evidence that television in the United States is compared to an eye and is often symbolized in ocular terms.

2. Evil effects are attributed to the television-eye: we summarize some of the dangers—actual or fantasized—connected with TV viewing.

3. We demonstrate the correspondence between the evil-eye belief of traditional cultures and videophobia in the United States, proposing several social and psychological reasons why television is often regarded as a malevolent force invading/damaging its viewers, their homes, and their society.

Television as Eye

Several books on television characterize the medium as an eye: Eddy's *Television, the Eye of Tomorrow* (1945); Metz's *Reflections in a Bloodshot Eye* (1975); Patterson and McClure's *The Unseeing Eye* (1976); and Paul's *The Hungry Eye* (1962). Dan Rather, heir to the throne of Walter Cronkite ("the most trusted man in America"), titled his recent book *The Camera Never Blinks* (1977). Edward R. Murrow's documentary series in the 1950s was called "See It Now," and innumerable local news programs proclaim that they present "eyewitness" news. The most prestigious television network (CBS), which so long dominated the ratings, boasts a stylized *eye* as its logo.

The word *television* literally means that the viewer sees at a distance, or *to* a distance. On the other hand, a distant vision comes *into* the home. It is not the viewers' own vision that is represented on the screen. Viewers may, in fact, look *outward;* but vision is mediated. In television, the viewers are represented by professional seers; their eyes are no longer their own.

The notion that the camera is an *eye* is as old as photography. From the start, the camera was both a means of looking *out*—an aggressive capture of the exterior world—and a relatively passive instrument for *receiving* pictures of reality. The Italian word *camera*, after all, means "room": the outside image penetrates into the darkened room (*camera obscura)* through a small window which opens onto the world. Photography both *takes* the outside in ("takes" pictures) and *accepts* the image of the outside; it is both active and passive.

In early film theory, the moving-picture camera was often compared to an eye. The concept reached its most advanced development in the writings of the Soviet filmmaker Dziga Vertov, who stressed photography as an action, rather than a passive activity. According to Vertov, the camera shoots pictures on the model of a gun—it is an assaulting, interventionist eye. The act of "looking" with a camera does not just reproduce the world, but activates and transforms the world. The gaze is never neutral. Yet today, most practitioners of documentary and commercial cinema prefer to regard cinema as a relatively passive reproduction of a real or fictional world, although theorists may argue the opposite. While there is still some concern over assault of the vulnerable eye/mind of an adolescent film viewer by pornographic cinema, censorship has decreased notably since the advent of television. In the movies today, almost anything goes. Yet the content of television is a subject of great moral concern. The point is that the rise of television as *the* mass entertainment medium coincided with an apparent decline of fear about the content of movies; simultaneously, the notion of cinema as an eye, still relatively undeveloped, was transferred to television. As fear of the new medium increased, the eye metaphor was adopted in popular and pseudo-academic literature.

Dangers Attributed to Television

The dangers of television viewing are alleged to be both physical and moral. For example, the U.S. Consumer Product Safety Commission in 1974 estimated that twelve thousand persons sustained television-related physical injuries during 1973 alone. These involved laceration (63 percent), contusion/abrasion (21 percent), and fractures (6 percent), *especially among children*. In addition, there are known cases of death by TV, due to electric shock, fire, and explosions. The commission claims that television is directly associated with 160 deaths a year. In-depth investigations by the U.S. Bureau of Epidemiology reveals cases such as these:

- At time of accident, victim was seated on a metal radiator with wet swim trunks on. When he reached over to the antennae to adjust the picture, he received a bolt which sent him through the picture window behind him.
- As victim pushed on-off switch with her cane, set burst into flames. Victim unplugged set, but fire spread to surroundings.
- Victim, who lives in a cluttered room, was injured when TV fell from a table as he walked past it.
- Victim most likely grabbed outside antennae pole and swung from porch to ground as she often did. She was found next to pole. An electrician called to the scene three hours after accident felt that the problem was in the TV set to which it was attached.

The U.S. government also is concerned about long-range biological harm as a result of radiation emitted by TV sets, in addition to immediate physical damage from shock and impact. The Food and Drug Administration administers an electronic radiation-control program mandated by Congress in 1968. According to the FDA:

> When the TV X-ray problem first became a public concern in 1966, the Surgeon General recommended that viewers sit at least six feet from an operating receiver to reduce the quite low potential of biological damage. Since that time, however, steps have been taken by both Government and industry to reduce further this exposure potential. There should now be no health hazard in watching TV at a distance at which the image quality is satisfactory to the viewer.

Having TV monitored by federal health-regulating agencies demonstrates the dimension of public concern. TV is popularly recognized for its addictive properties, witnessed vividly by the book *The Plug-In Drug* (Winn, 1977) and by personal reports by people who stopped watching for one month in return for $500 from the *Detroit Free Press* in 1977. Some of the temporary "nonviewers" said, after their abstinence period:

> I just feel drawn to the TV.
>
> I thought I'd go crazy.
>
> It was like cutting off the gas.
>
> [*Detroit Free Press*, November 6, 1977, p. 10-A]

Research shows that, when television is watched heavily, there are a number of direct threats to health and well-being. For example, heavy viewers sleep less and are less active in social, educational, and athletic organizations. Heavy viewers are more pessimistic about the future, often saying it would be unfair to bring children into the world. Children who view heavily are in turn likely to say that people can't be trusted and that you must be careful in dealing with others. Among very young viewers (preschoolers), some have been impaired even by the most conscientiously designed children's program, "Sesame Street," so much so that direct clinical intervention was necessary, in the experience of Werner Halpern:

> The jived up repetitious auditory and visual experience evidently may be too much for some children to assimilate or to avoid successfully. When their nervous systems become overtaxed, they resort to diffuse tension and discharge behaviors exemplified by unforced hyperactivity and irritability. In animal research at least, younger creatures are more susceptible to the diminution of adaptive capacities in the face of stress and to the induction of neuroses than are older ones. A similar condition for children points to the possibility that sensory overload may precipitate more than transient behavior problems [*Journal of Communications,* no. 25, Fall 1975].

In the 1977 trial of Ronnie Zamora, accused of first-degree murder in Miami, Florida, the defense lawyer argued that Zamora was driven insane by "prolonged sublimal television intoxication." Zamora was said to be intoxicated particularly by "Kojak" and "Police Woman"; according to the defense, "Without the influence of television, there would have been no crime." However, testimony of a psychiatrist that purported to prove a positive association between television violence and aggressive behavior in children was excluded by the court when the witness was unable to state that the evidence demonstrated a direct link between television and any given homicide. In his closing argument, the prosecutor ridiculed the claim that television inspired a murder. The jury apparently agreed with the prosecutor. Ronnie Zamora was found guilty of murder in the first degree. Television was presumably absolved of the crime.

One of the most notorious opponents of television is Frederic Wertham, a psychiatrist who has attempted to link violence on television with riots, gang warfare, and the rise in street crime, a theme echoed in the sixties by John Pastore, chairman of the Senate Communication Subcommittee, and by the surgeon general of the United States. In his book of 1954, *Seduction of the Innocent,* Wertham wrote:

> The relentless commercialism and the surfeit of brutality, violence, and sadism has made a profound impression on susceptible young people. The result is a distortion of natural attitudes in the direction of cynicism, greed, hostility, callousness, and insensitivity. . . . Harmful mass media influences are a contributing factor in many young people's troubles.

Similarly, Harry Skornia, in his influential summary of behaviorist literature on TV, *Television and Society,* warns of potentially dire effects of viewing:

> . . . the way in which our media create and wield masses is strangely disquieting and ominous. Only thirty years ago masses assembled in the sports [arenas] in Nuremberg and Berlin, shouting "Sieg heil" with spine-chilling monotony.

The Evil Eye and Videophobia

The belief that one can harm another's property or person simply by looking at it with an "evil" gaze is found throughout Europe, the Near East, North and East Africa, Indonesia, the Caribbean, and parts of Japan and South America. Maloney, et al., document that in the United States, variations of this traditional belief existed primarily in Hispanic communities and among the descendants of immigrants from Central Europe and the Mediterranean cultures. The older generation of Slovak-Americans still displays strong forms of the belief. Many anthropologists believe that fear of the eye spread from the Middle East and was diffused into Latin America by the Spanish. Belief in the evil eye has been discovered as early as ancient Egypt, where the eye was considered the window of the soul and the means of access to it. In a moment of anger, the god Osiris could destroy with a glance. Hebrew culture was pervaded by the fear of the destructive gaze. "Eat not the bread of him that hath an evil eye," warns the book of Proverbs (23:6). Even one of the Ten Commandments has been interpreted as an injunction against casting the evil eye: "You shall not covet your neighbor's house: you shall not covet your neighbor's wife, or his manservant, or his maidservant, or his ox, or his ass, or anything that is your neighbor's" (Exodus 20:17). At least through the Renaissance,

European Christians viewed the Jews as the source of the evil eye. Canon Law 49 of the Council of Elvira forbade Jews to stand among the ripening crops of Christians "lest they cause the crops to rot and wither with their malevolent glances." The Jews of England were forbidden to attend the coronation of Richard the Lion-Hearted for fear that an evil eye might harm the crown. A German word for evil eye to this day remains *Judenblick,* the Jews' glance.

Sometimes called "overlooking" by anthropologists, the evil eye is not always intended to harm. The destructive glance may be cast unwittingly, as when strangers in Mexico admire children with too much enthusiasm. In India and Iran and among Slovak-Americans, the eye may be cast by a member of one's family, including one's mother. Or the glances of friends may ruin a prized possession. Clarence Maloney reports in *The Evil Eye* that an Indian family in Washington, D.C., owned a parrot that was trained to say the names of many people. One day, friends dropped by and commented favorably on the parrot, and that very afternoon it dropped dead.

As in the case of the Indian family just cited, belief in the insidious powers of the fixed gaze (expressing admiration or envy) is sometimes combined with fear of destruction by way of mouth. Complimentary words which accompany the admiring glance may kill a parrot, curdle milk, sicken a child, ruin a dinner under preparation. Anthropologists consider the Filipino belief in the baleful effect of the admiring word, called the "hot mouth," to be a variant of the evil-eye belief. Yet, whenever the bad or hot mouth and the evil eye are found in association, the power of the eye is usually believed to be stronger.

It is interesting to note, in reference to the hot mouth, that, although U.S. television is most regarded as a form of seeing, the camera eye is characterized also in oral terms. The medium is said to have an endless "appetite" for new material, which it presumably destroys through the production process.

The evil eye is usually cast by strangers, according to the traditional Old World belief. In Italy, those with bloodshot eyes are particularly suspect. Sometimes a deity or a devil is the source of the gaze. But among Slovak-Americans and Mexicans, evil emanations can pervade the whole environment, surrounding victims from all directions. As Elworthy (1958) states, in his classic nineteenth-century study *The Evil Eye:*

> When anyone looks at what is excellent with an envious eye, he fills the surrounding atmosphere with a pernicious quality, and transmits his own envenomed exhalations into whatever is nearest to him.

In Italy, the evil eye is compared to an all-pervasive virus or plague. In Mexico, the effects of a generalized "bad air" are often undistinguishable from the evil effects of a specifically located *mal de ojo* or "bad eye." Mexicans also liken the evil eye to a destructive charge of electricity (again, note the parallel to TV). The victims of *mal de ojo* in its electrical form do not so much die from sudden shock as gradually sicken, dry up, wither way, as from a form of radiation sickness. The Mexican fear of *electricidad* thus seems analogous to the American belief in the harmful effects of microwave transmissions and the related fear of living under or near high-voltage transmission lines (which provide power for TV, among other appliances).

People who fear or suspect that the evil eye will ruin their possessions or members of their family customarily take protective measures. The most common forms of defense (called "gaze prophylaxis") involve wearing charms or amulets on the body, hanging them on doors, making signs with the hand, asking a deity for protection, and crossing oneself. Some charms display an eye—usually a blue eye—to look back at the bearer of the destructive gaze. It may be intended to reflect the evil gaze back at the gazer or merely to oppose the gaze with a countergaze. In any case, the protective charm is meant to reflect, deflect, or absorb the evil eye's glance. In Mexico, a large brown seed known as *ojo de venado* ("deer's eye") is commonly used as protection, along with pictures of "Our Lady." Other common charms include small, twisted, red plastic *cuernos* ("horns") and pieces of red yarn. Gold, silver, and amber are among the materials believed to be particularly effective against the evil eye. In the northern Adriatic, fishing boats are painted with a large eye on the prow which is identified with Santa Chiara (St. Claire of Assisi). Santa Chiara not only possesses the ability to aid victims of the evil eye, but *she is also the patron saint of television*. (In the United States, we note several types of "charms" used in conjunction with TV. Threatening black leopards may prowl the set. Benign graduation photos may be arranged on top. A votive Lava Lite may burn nearby.)

The television viewer typically *meets* the eye of the people who inhabit the screen. In the theatrical film experience, by contrast, actors look at each other but do not explicitly recognize the existence of the offscreen audience. The actors act as if the audience simply does not exist. The prohibition "do not look at the camera" appears to be based on the idea that the exchange of a look would break the illusion of reality, thus destroying the magic of the movie experience by forcibly reminding spectators that they are only outsiders looking at the image of actors who are only pretending.

On the other hand, the normal TV viewing experiences involve prolonged, direct eye-to-eye contact between spectators and newscasters, comedians, preachers, teachers, hucksters, politicians, and talk-show hosts. Interviewees are commanded to look directly at the TV camera. The direct gaze at the spectator from the TV presumably establishes the reality of the experience. Television tries to appear unmediated—a sending eye not only *witnessing* reality, but affirming the presence of the receiving eye. In turn, the spectator plays the role of a watching eye, witnessing the transmitting vision. The viewing eye acknowledges the truth of the TV message by meeting its eye, one on one, in an exchange of looks.

Although TV *fictions* usually obey the feature film rule that there should be no eye contact between performer and spectator, these stories are broken every twelve or fifteen minutes by sales pitches in which performers who display products attempt to engage viewers in a reciprocal exchange of looks. The entertaining fiction is collapsed into commercial reality by means of the same direct gaze that is used to underline the presumed reality of the news. Our point, then, is that much of television, though not all of it, purports to be reality and that the sense of reality is founded on eye-to-eye contact between sender and receiver.

The communication of television is almost always a one-way flow, from the set to a viewer who is denied the possibility of immediately replying to the message. Within this context of the one-way flow, there is every reason to believe that any eye contact between the performer and viewer can be unconsciously understood as an aggressive look that is trying to influence viewers (specifically, to part with their time and money). It is a look that demands something and at the same time covets the audience's continued attention.

It is well known that many parents use television as a babysitter. TV diverts and amuses children, keeping them quiet. Children *watch* television; but, in effect, they are *being watched* by a parent substitute.

But is TV the benevolent eye parents wish it to be? In this context, consider the public-service announcement shown on late-night TV in Cleveland: Several children were asked by an off-camera presence, "If you had to give up TV or give up talking with your father, which would you choose? The TV or your father?" Each child states, quite charmingly, yet firmly, that he or she would give up Dad. Then printed across the screen is the warning "Use Television, Don't Abuse It." These words "use, don't abuse" are usually connected with drugs.

We should remember at this point that the most vulnerable victims of the evil eye in most cultures are precisely children. In the public-service announcement above, television is explicitly cast in the role of *rival* to the parent. Television, the substitute parent, presumably has stolen the child's love from the real parent. The benevolent babysitter is actually a thief; it has destroyed the natural love relationship between parent and child. The ad directly invites "me" (the addressee) to be jealous of the medium that has taken the love of one who once loved me or who is supposed to love me. Indirectly, it blames the parent for failing to protect the child from the insidious effects of television; yet it offers me the opportunity to blame TV, not myself, for my child's failure to love me.

An elementary psychological analysis of the public-service announcement suggests the following: The parents are presented with the shocking spectacle of the unloving child. Although these children do not love their parents, it is essential to the role of the "good parent" that parents *must* love their children. They cannot regard them as hateful beings; they cannot blame their children for failure to love, but neither does the ad directly blame the parents for losing the children's love. Instead, it invites them to blame the perversion of a normal love relationship on a third party—television. The parents' failure to hold and strengthen the child's love is seen not so much as the fault of the parent as that of the tube itself. The public-service announcement invites the parents to project their guilt onto the television set, transforming the medium from a protective eye to a love-thief. The parents project qualities they prefer not to recognize in themselves onto an instrument they previously considered harmless or neutral. Television becomes an externalized, repudiated *bad self;* TV, in other words, is the bad mother, the bad father, absolving the parents of all crimes but neglect.

If the public-service announcement above is effective, it will succeed in alarming parents to a situation of evil and inspire them to take action to break children of the TV habit. In short, a second weaning is required. It is interesting to note in this context that Slovak-Americans believe that a sickly or evil child is a product of indecisive weaning practices. The Slovak tradition asserts that one should withdraw the breast firmly, once and for all, or suffer an unnatural child. The public-service announcement suggests, in turn, that television is commonly used in the American home to nurture the child in lieu of parental attention, while Ellison's provocative title *The Glass Teat* (1970) suggests that TV functions precisely as a mother's breast that comforts and feeds (in this case, both children and adults). The implication is that watching television, like breast feeding, is a regressive activity antagonistic to the natural process of growing up. According to the public-service announcement, the child who watches too much TV unnaturally withholds love from parents, redirecting it onto the parental substitute. The parent must break this dependence, must discipline the child, through a process of limitation or prohibition, thereby regaining the child's love. As in weaning or toilet-training, firmness is required, not for the parent's sake, but "for the good of the children."

In any jealous struggle for possession, according to Susan Isaacs (1949), "a thing that has long been treated with indifference or contempt by the owner may suddenly assume great value in his eyes if another person begins to desire it." Envy, Isaacs asserts, is in "intimate relation with the motives of power, of rivalry, of guilt, and of love." What the parents previously took for granted (children's love, the TV set) achieves a supreme importance once they fear that their children are being "possessed" by the eye of television.

The word *envy* is derived from the Latin word *invidia,* signifying a destructive emanation or *projection* of an eye outwards toward the possessions or good fortune of others. The evil eye is traditionally associated with envious, jealous, or covetous behavior. Francis Bacon wrote (1597): "We understand why The Bible called envy the evil eye, for in the act of envy there is an ejaculation or irradiation of an eye." He who casts the evil eye admires my beautiful child, my ox, my pottery, wishing to possess them. As Bacon expressed this in a finely turned phrase: "Envy is as the sunbeams, that beat hotter upon a back or a steep rising ground than upon a flat." When the gazer is unable to seize the superior possessions, he or she (or it) destroys or sickens them with a glance, ensuring that the other will no longer enjoy the envied good fortune.

As we argue that television is regarded as an evil eye, we of course cannot ignore the fact that commercial television is founded on advertising explicitly intended to inspire the viewers to buy—thus possess—products and life-styles that are enjoyed by others on the screen. Advertisers try to convince viewers that they need certain products in order to enjoy the pleasure, happy times, and good fortune of those who display, and presumably use, certain products. In other words, commercial television succeeds or fails, economically, by catalyzing covetousness in viewers, creating desire for products by first inspiring envy toward those persons on TV who enjoy the "good life."

The eye of television looks outward, at a world both real and fictional. Yet, our evidence suggests that viewers, moralists, and researchers believe that the eye also gazes inward, into the home, maliciously influencing or actually injuring its viewers, physically and morally. In both the evil-eye tradition and in television "effects" research, children are assumed to be primary victims of a malignant, acquisitive vision.

It is noteworthy that television itself warns viewers that its programs "may not be suitable for children; parental discretion is advised." Or, more explicitly, "The producers of 'Odyssey' warn that you may find this program objectionable"—that it might assault both the eye and morals even of adult viewers. Here, the spoken and printed warning functions much like the gaze prophylaxis mentioned above, in which a possessor of the evil eye acknowledges the fears of the gazee. Although the gazer (in this case, TV) proclaims by its warning that he/she/it does not intend to cast a destructive gaze, those who receive the glance are nevertheless advised to protect themselves, their children, and their wealth.

APPENDIX
Interview with Garry Marshall

Executive producer-director-writer Garry Marshall was born in New York City, November 13, 1934. He graduated from Northwestern University with a B.A. in journalism in 1956. While at the university, Garry formed a jazz combo which played in Chicago clubs and hotels.

After college, Marshall served in Korea as production chief of the Armed Forces Radio Network. He wrote, produced, and performed on Korean television.

Following the war, Marshall began at the *New York Daily News* as a copy boy. While working his way up to by-lined reporter, he also formed a new jazz combo to play clubs in New York and New Jersey. At the same time, he wrote for comedians Phil Foster and Joey Bishop.

In 1960, Bishop and Foster recommended him to Jack Paar, and Garry left the *Daily News* to join Paar's writing staff for the old "Tonight Show." In 1962, he went to Hollywood to write for Joey Bishop's new comedy series.

A year later, Marshall teamed up with Joey Belson; and, in 1964, the duo wrote over 100 television segments, including episodes for "The Danny Thomas Show," "The Lucy Show" (20 episodes), and the old "Dick Van Dyke Show" (25 episodes). For the Dick Van Dyke series, they won writing awards, including the Emmy. Besides comedy, they wrote segments for "I Spy" and the "Chrysler Presents" dramatic series.

In 1965, the duo created their own comedy series, "Hey, Landlord," which ran on NBC for a year. In 1967, Marshall and Belson wrote and produced their first movie, *How Sweet It Is,* a comedy with Debbie

Reynolds and James Garner. The following year, they wrote and produced *The Grasshopper,* which starred Jacqueline Bisset.

In 1969, they again teamed up to develop "The Odd Couple," which Garry produced during its five-year run on ABC television. In 1972, Marshall created the "Little People" series for NBC, which starred Brian Keith and was filmed in Hawaii. It ran two years. In January, 1973, Marshall created "Happy Days," which is still running at this writing.

In 1976, he created "Laverne and Shirley," which debuted with the highest Nielsen ratings in the last TV decade. Marshall's sister Penny, who also appeared in "The Odd Couple," plays one of the leads, Laverne. Behind the scenes, Garry's father Tony acts as producer for the show, while another sister, Ronnie Hallin, is associate producer for "Happy Days."

More recent Marshall productions include: "Mork and Mindy," "Joanie Loves Chachi," "The New Odd Couple," and the 1983 theatrically released film *Young Doctors in Love,* which Marshall also directed.

The following conversation between Marshall and Stuart Kaminsky took place in October, 1979.

Kaminsky: When you sit down to write or produce a comedy show, do you say, "I'm going to do a certain kind of comedy"?

Marshall: Definitely, yes. In "The Odd Couple," I created a certain kind of sophisticated comedy, kind of drawing-room comedy, heavy on the dialogue and repartee, an adult kind of humor. If we picked up kids, fine. In "Happy Days," I was trying to upgrade what was called the traditional family comedy, the "Donna Reed," "Father Knows Best' sort of thing. I felt you could make those shows funnier and still have what was called the family comedy. We wanted to play a kind of double-level comedy; on one level, for adults in the sense of a warm, interesting comedy; and on the other, for the children.

Kaminsky: So when you had the original idea for "Happy Days," you were thinking in terms of family comedy, and you did have in mind some of the things that you were reacting against and trying to take a step further.

Marshall: When I started "Happy Days," it was done almost as a personal vendetta, to do a show that parents and children could watch together. I have three children, and I had a lot of trouble finding something to watch with them. The best thing was to take them to a Disney movie, but I was getting tired of watching a raccoon lick a duck for an hour and a half.

Kaminsky: When you decided what the family was going to be like on "Happy Days," were you looking at other shows, or were you deciding what kinds of variations you could play within the family?

Marshall: Well, in any series, the two-people "rub" is the best "rub." This comes from "The Odd Couple." It's the focus on the two that I was interested in, rather than one. On "The Mary Tyler Moore Show," she was pitted variously against each character. I wanted the two, which is a different concept; but I wasn't sure which the two would be. I knew one was Richie. I played with Richie and Potsie as two best friends, but that didn't work too well. The Potsie character wasn't cooking. And then I was going to try Richie with the younger sister, but the younger sister wasn't a good enough actress; so, as it turned out, the two push came with Richie and Fonzie; that became a Tom Sawyer–Huckleberry Finn concept, and that worked, and it carried the show. I would have taken any two; I just couldn't find the other match to Richie, and then Fonzie matched.

Kaminsky: That match didn't even take place until fairly late, until the second season.

Marshall: Yes, that's right. In the first year and a half, I was still finding where the match was. One of the keys to comedy is realizing when you're not doing it right. You change and make an adjustment.

Kaminsky: One thing else I've noticed about your shows is you start with a small group; and then, as the series continues, you expand the group.

Marshall: Yes, that's traditional television casting. The network (ABC) prefers five. Eight seems to work better as protection.

Kaminsky: In a pilot produced by you, "Beans in Boston," you started with nine characters right away.

Marshall: But that wasn't pure Garry Marshall. Actually "Beans in Boston" was a show created by two guys in England who couldn't get it on American television unless I put my name on it. So I saw what they did, adjusted their show slightly to fit American television, and then let them go. I really had little to do with it. There are a number of shows I've had a lot to do with, such as "The Odd Couple," "Happy Days," "Laverne and Shirley," and "Mork and Mindy." On "Laverne

Garry Marshall

The cast and crew of "Laverne and Shirley."

and Shirley," I was specifically trying to replace "Lucy." There was nobody doing low physical comedy on television. I figured there was a big opening for that if I could do it with girls. I was definitely looking for low physical comedy on ''Laverne and Shirley,'' which we got. It's probably the only show that still does this comedy. And in "Mork and Mindy," I was exploring the far-out, off-the-wall comedy that was again becoming popular and trying to prove that you could do a satirical, off-the-wall comedy like "Saturday Night Live" at eight o'clock. I said if I could get the right actor, I could do it; and we've managed to do it, and it was quite successful.

Kaminsky: "Mork and Mindy" did all those new things; but, in another sense, it goes all the way back to the single comedian who, like Chaplin or Keaton, is sort of out of touch with his society. He wants to be a part of it but just can't make it. He always wants to be integrated into society, and society won't take him in.

Marshall: I must say I didn't particularly have that in mind, other than I was a big student and fan of Chaplin and Keaton and the "isolated man" in the sense I think that's a good character. I wasn't conscious of it with "Mork and Mindy." In Chaplin, it was the isolated man who couldn't adjust to society, and he was wrong and felt out of place. "Mork and Mindy" is the reverse. I wanted to have a man from another planet coming down and saying, "You're all crazy, folks. This society is wrong; I'm right; this society is wrong," even though he's trying to adjust. It's the Chaplin above, rather than below. We play the comedy as the lost soul walking around, but the theoretical attitude underneath Mork is his observation of our society and pointing out how crazy it is. Examination of comedy, all in all, is very complex. I think Robin Williams and my sister Penny are two great clowns, Ronny Howard, Henry Winkler are very fine comedy actors, while Cindy Williams is a very fine improvisational actress. In this era of television, the performer is more important than the actor. Today, you need immediate impact, and a performer is usually more powerful than an actor; the impact is faster. It is not better, just faster. You can get a verdict from an audience more quickly on a performer than on an actor. It's the era of the performer; and if you get performers, you've got to write *to* them. If you get a good clown, write to the clown. If he's not a clown, don't write clown.

Kaminsky: You said your sister is a comic performer and Cindy Williams is an actress. I think that shows up in the stories, too. Quite often, Shirley starts getting involved in courtship situations, interrelationships with another character, whereas Laverne, although that sometimes happens with her, too, continues playing on her comic character.

Marshall: Just making people laugh is not good enough; it never has been good enough. You have to make them come back again. If you're doing one show, it's all right; but on television, to make people come back, you have to have some relationship working. You're selling love. It's as simple as that. You must love the character; and if they're just funny, you don't necessarily love the character. You laugh to make the audience laugh, and then you have to have some sort of relationship comedy underneath to make them love. Penny will start as a total clown. She'll do ten minutes of having her hand stuck in an urn. That's totally clown; but later, at the end, she'll put her arm around Cindy, and they'll say, all right, listen, you're okay, I'm okay, we'll survive together, we're friends, and they'll go off together.

Kaminsky: When you're writing scripts, do you ever get to a point where the characters start talking for themselves, write themselves?

Marshall: Many times in a given situation if you've got it down, the characters will write themselves. You have to punch it up, but basically the characters will take you right through the scene. You have to write attitudes for the characters. Usually, then you're not at a loss how to write them in a given situation.

Kaminsky: So much of what you do is within a half-hour format. Do you find yourself just thinking in half hours? Or twenty-six minutes, etc.?

Marshall: Yes; no question about it. I'm doing a screenplay now, and I've got to adjust my mind to a screenplay. For the past two years, every morning, I was with my partner, we were writing a play, and then in the afternoon, I went back into television. It was a big adjustment. In the afternoons, my mind would go into a twenty-six-minute format. No question. And after you do a thousand half hours, you get a clock in your stomach that tells you where the twenty-six minutes are. If you give me a story idea, I'll tell you if it'll fit. So you do get to master a thing, and some people master it so well they can't do anything else.

Kaminsky: It's hard to break out of.

Marshall: Yes, usually when we're seeing if we have a show, we're looking for a beginning, a middle, curtain, commercial, a little "catch" curtain line at the midway point, and three quarters of the way, a block scene, meaning a big comedy scene, and then a few minutes left to say we have a relationship here. Lucy used to do a block scene at three quarters and take it on out. And that was it. We did a block scene on "Laverne and Shirley" at three quarters, stopped, and had two minutes of hey, we're real people, we have feelings, we have pain, and we're friends, take it on out.

Kaminsky: Several of your series—"Laverne and Shirley," "Mork and Mindy"—have been spin-offs from "Happy Days."

Marshall: In television shows, you want to have people to do spin-offs for another show. So while you're juggling a main show, you're also bringing characters up within the same twenty-six minutes, so they can spin off with their own program. That's very hard. Many creators and writers have problems with that, but it's a network push. I've taken a new approach to the whole thing. I do my main show, and then I bring in an outside character in an episode or two, and then spin them off rather than spinning off my main cast[1]. That's how I got "Laverne and Shirley" and "Mork and Mindy," both came off "Happy Days." I did this rather than spin off my own guys; the network kept insisting I should do it, but I don't think it works.

Kaminsky: One thing I've noticed quite often in television comedy is the idea of moving people out. The idea of "We're gonna take them on a trip—we're gonna take them to China; we're gonna take them someplace else."

Marshall: Yes, that's when a show is getting stale. It's not moving around. Nowadays, you still run into that problem. "Happy Days" is going into its seventh year. What we do now is, usually to kick off the year, we try to move them out someplace if we can for just an opening. "Happy Days" went to New York; "Happy Days" went to a dude ranch or something. All we do is one episode, an hour episode a year. We're up to 145 episodes of "Happy Days," maybe 150, so you've got to start hyping with some new character and sometimes some movement. I agree with what you were just saying, but it doesn't necessarily have to be stated negatively. Moving out can also be more interesting. But it's a dead giveaway that we're groping for ideas; there's no question about that.

---

[1] Subsequent to this interview Marshall changed his practice with "Joanie Loves Chachi."

Kaminsky: As you get more and more episodes, one problem you have to deal with is whether you're going to remember what happened before, whether you want to have a sort of consistency, or whether each episode's a new world and you forget about the part. Each of your shows seems to treat that a little differently.

Marshall: Yes, it's a problem. Staffs of shows change. You've got to keep bringing in fresh writers. Writers get tired, and they switch to other shows. So it's traditional to keep one writer on all the way who becomes a historian for the show. We have one on "Happy Days," one on "Laverne and Shirley." And sometimes it's a writer you don't even want anymore, but you have no historian. You need one person staying there who remembers what happened in the past. Sometimes you make big mistakes, but a lot of times you try for accuracy. Fonzie has jumped from running away from home when he was six to running away from home when he was three to running away from home when he was nine. Just sloppiness on the part of the historian. We try to do it right. Sometimes you just make mistakes.

Kaminsky: It seems to me that, as a series goes on longer and longer, one of the things the fans like is that historical reference.

Marshall: Fans usually were right in telling when we made a mistake of that type. "The Odd Couple," it seems to me, was pretty accurate. Tony Randall became the historian. Once he forgot Felix's brother's name. He had a brother in Buffalo. We couldn't remember his name; we had to go looking up old scripts to find out what the hell his name was.

Kaminsky: In any of your shows, have you ever actually had someone sit down and write the history? Have a book on it?

Marshall: No, but each show has what you call a synopsis sheet. In other words, every episode ever done is written up in a paragraph and kept in a file. That's usually for new writers who come in. We show them five years of a show so that they don't come up with the same stories. Within these synopses are usually good histories. But sometimes, to find names and characters, you have to go back and look at the script. There's a newsman in Rhode Island who has taken "The Odd Couple" as a kind of cult show in reruns, and twice in his paper he's given an "Odd Couple" trivia test. Two of the show's writers took the test and failed.

Kaminsky: What do you think is a reasonable time for someone to come up with a script? How long do you think a writer should take?

Marshall: With "Mork and Mindy," I took eight writers down to Palm Springs for three days. Every day, we sat around together, pitched story areas, and laid out stories. Pretty soon, beginnings, middles, and ends came. Then we put all the stories in a pot. At the end of three days, I said, "I'll take these two; you take these two; you take these two. . . ." There's always one story that nobody wants to write, because they know it doesn't really work. They say it's too hard. The producer has to end up writing that one. Then, within two weeks at the most, they come back with their first drafts. I let them rewrite, and then they come back in three or four days with the second draft. Then I put it into mimeo, and we rehearse it five days, polishing, changing, switching. Then we shoot it. That's the traditional way. Of course, maybe in television, because of the stupidity of the business, you don't always have that much time. Many of the staff write scripts overnight or on a weekend. For the free-lancer, it's simple. He comes in. We talk about ideas. I send him off to block it out. He blocks it out on a three-, four-page outline; and then we go over his outline. That takes a day, two days. We go over his outline, change it, and then say, "Forget it; this isn't going to work." Sometimes we just end up paying for the outline, or we say, "This will work," and let him go to the script. It's all done in steps with free-lancing. He goes and writes the first draft. If you're in a big hurry, you say, "I need it in a week." If you're not, you say, "Two weeks," two weeks being the average. Money has changed it. When I was a free-lancer, I used to take two, three weeks to write a script and really try to write it well. Free-lancers now kind of rush, go too fast. To make money, they have to do so many scripts a year. I must admit, my partner Jerry Belson and I hold the record for speed—in 1965, we wrote thirty-six one-half-hour comedy scripts. That's the record for free-lancing.

Kaminsky: Based on your own stories?

Marshall: Yes. The thirty-six scripts were spread over five or six different shows. Sidney Sheldon used to write all the "I Dream of Jeannie"s, Jerry and I had no show. It was strictly free-lances off the street. The reason we did that that year was to get enough money so that the next year we wrote only two scripts for existing series and created all our own shows, because we had enough money, and we didn't have to write. Free-lancers get sloppy, mostly for money reasons.

Kaminsky: Do you watch other people's shows?

Marshall: Yes, I watch all the new shows; and once in a while, I will check other shows for various reasons. I watch “Barney Miller” a lot because “Barney Miller” has some of the best casting in television. I steal people off that show; I see a character, and I hire him to be in my show. I watched “All in the Family” because my brother-in-law [Rob Reiner] was on it. “M*A*S*H” I check once in a while. I watch all sports, and I like dramatic shows from time to time. I like the specials. When I can, I watch. I’m not an addict, but I enjoy it.

BIBLIOGRAPHY

Atkin, Charles. *Television And Social Behavior: An Annotated Bibliography of Research Focusing on Television's Impact on Children.* Rockford, Maryland: National Institute of Mental Health, 1971.

Bacon, Francis: "Of Envy," in *Essays, Civil and Moral.* 1597. Reprinted in The Harvard Classics, edited by Charles W. Eliot, Vol. 3. New York: P. F. Collier & Son, 1909.

Berger, Thomas. *Arthur Rex: A Legendary Novel.* New York: Delacorte Press/Seymour Lawrence, 1978.

Blair, Karen. *Meaning in Star Trek.* Chambersburg, Pennsylvania: Anima Books, 1977.

Carr, Edward H. *What Is History?* New York: Alfred A. Knopf, 1962.

Cawelti, John G. *Adventure, Mystery and Romance.* Chicago: University of Chicago Press, 1976.

Comstock, George, et al. *Television and Human Behavior.* New York: Columbia University Press, 1978.

Eddy, William C. *Television, the Eye of Tomorrow.* New York: Prentice-Hall, 1945.

Eliade, Mircea. *Myth and Reality.* New York: Harper Colophon Books, 1975.

Ellison, Harlan. *The Glass Teat: Essays of Opinion on the Subject of Television.* New York: Pyramid Books, 1975.

Elworthy, Frederic Thomas. *The Evil Eye.* London: J. Murray, 1958.

Erikson, Erik H. "Ritualization in Everyday Life." *Toys and Reason: Stages in the Ritualization of Experience.* New York: W. W. Norton, 1977.

Fiske, John, and Hartley, John. *Reading Television.* London: Methuen, 1978.

Foucault, Michel. *The Order of Things*. New York: Random House, 1970.

Freud, Sigmund. *Civilization and Its Discontents*. New York: W. W. Norton, 1961.

Freud, Sigmund. *Totem and Taboo*. New York: W. W. Norton, 1950.

Frye, Northrop. *Anatomy of Criticism*. Princeton, New Jersey: Princeton University Press, 1957.

Isaacs, Susan. "Property and Possessiveness." *Childhood and After*. New York: International Universities Press, 1949.

Jung, Carl G., ed. *Man and His Symbols*. London: Aldus Books, 1964.

Kaminsky, Stuart M. *American Film Genres*. Chicago: Nelson-Hall, 1984.

Koestler, Arthur. *The Sleepwalkers*. New York: Macmillan, 1968.

MacDonald, J. Fred. *Blacks and White TV: Afro-Americans in Television since 1948*. Chicago: Nelson-Hall, 1983.

Maloney, Clarence. *The Evil Eye*. New York: Columbia University Press, 1976.

Metz, Robert. *CBS: Reflections in a Bloodshot Eye*. Chicago: Playboy Press, 1975.

Patterson, Thomas E., and McClure, Robert D. *The Unseeing Eye*. New York: Putnam, 1976.

Paul, Eugene. *The Hungry Eye*. New York: Valentine, 1963.

Propp, Vladimir. *The Morphology of the Folktale*. Austin: University of Texas Press, 1971.

Rather, Dan. *The Camera Never Blinks*. New York: William Morrow, 1977.

Skornia, Harry Jay. *Television and Society: An Inquest and Agenda for Improvement*. New York: McGraw-Hill, 1965.

Slothin, Richard. *Regeneration through Violence*. Middletown, Conn.: Wesleyan University Press, 1973.

Wertham, Frederic. *Seduction of the Innocent*. New York: Rinehart, 1954.

Winn, Marie. *Plug-in Drug*. New York: Viking Press, 1977.

INDEX